Logos That Last: How to Create Iconic Visual Branding

Left Page:
PDCo Ampersand Print
2020

Logos That Last: How to Create Iconic Visual Branding
by Allan Peters

ROCKPORT

This book is dedicated to my wife, Maria.
Thank you for inspiring me.
Thank you for loving me.
Thank you for fighting for me.
Thank you for making me a better man.
I'm so thankful for you.

Quarto.com

© 2023 Quarto Publishing Group USA Inc.
Text, Illustrations © 2023 Peters Design Company, PetersDesignCompany.com

First published in 2023 by Rockport Publishers, an imprint of The Quarto Group,
100 Cummings Center, Suite 265-D, Beverly, MA 01915, USA.
T (978) 282-9590 F (978) 283-2742

Rockport Publishers titles are also available at discount for retail, wholesale, promotional, and bulk purchase. For details, contact the Special Sales Manager by email at specialsales@quarto.com or by mail at The Quarto Group, Attn: Special Sales Manager, 100 Cummings Center, Suite 265-D, Beverly, MA 01915, USA.

10 9 8 7 6 5

ISBN: 978-0-7603-8317-9

Digital edition published in 2023
eISBN: 978-0-7603-8318-6

Library of Congress Cataloging-in-Publication Data available

Design: Allan Peters
Cover Image: Allan Peters
Page Layout: Allan Peters
Photography: Allan Peters, Maria Peters, TC Worley, Freadom, Right Way Signs, Mark Peters, Wits, City of Eagan, Adam Hoganson
Illustration: Allan Peters

Printed in China

Contents

7   Hello
9   The Pursuit of Perfection
12 The Beginning

18 **Chapter 1: What Makes a Logo Last?**
41 **Chapter 2: Brand Mark Process**
69 **Chapter 3: Inspiration Hunting**
80 **Chapter 4: Badge Design Process**
92 **Chapter 5: Brand Extensions**
104 **Chapter 6: Brand Evolution**
120 **Chapter 7: The Shop**
128 **Chapter 8: Case Studies**
182 **Chapter 9: Passion Projects**

203 Thank You
204 Acknowledgments
204 About the Author
206 Index

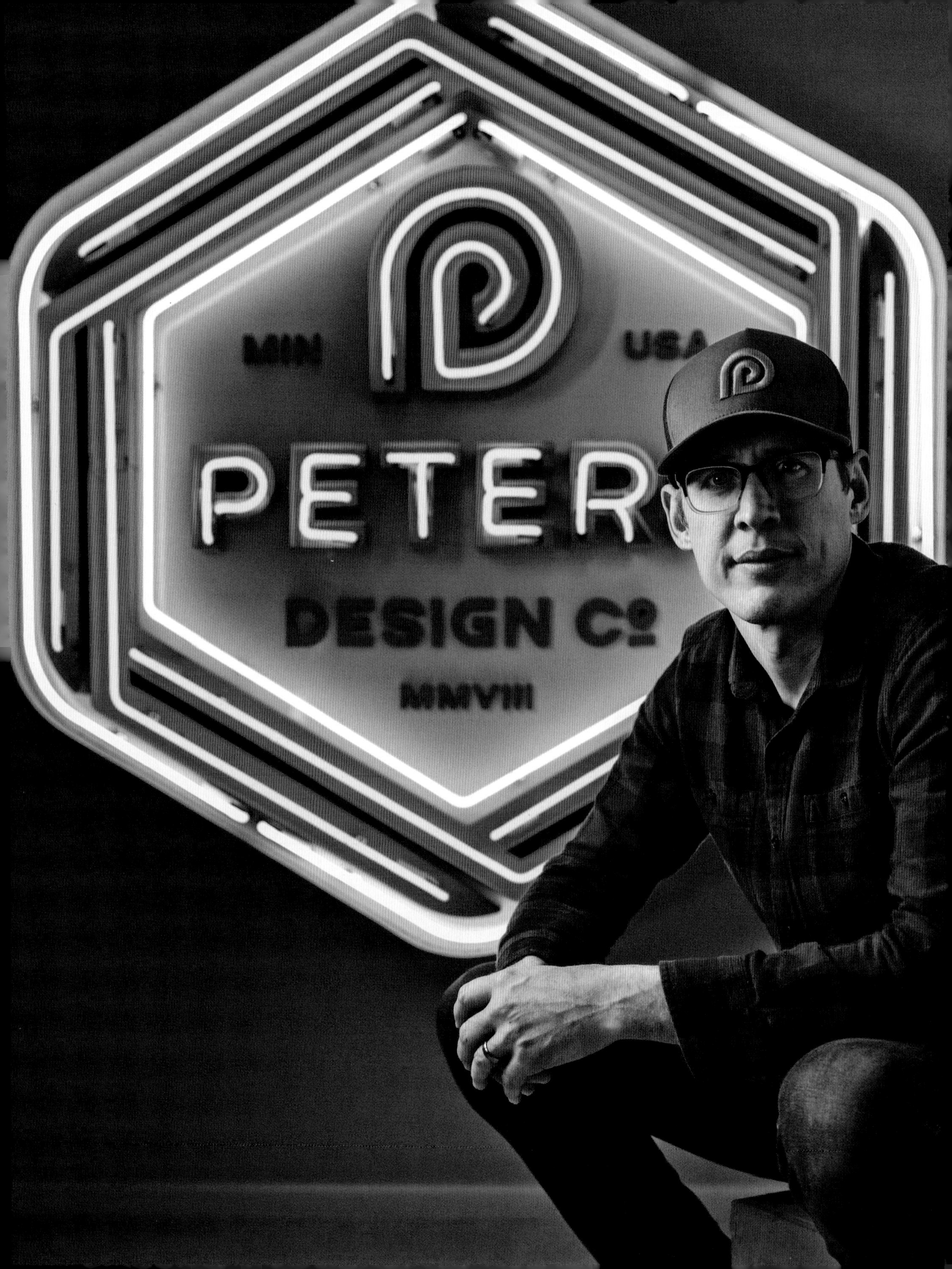
MN
USA
PETER
DESIGN Co
MMVIII

Hello

When I was in my twenties, I'd work late nights all the time. Not because I had to. I did it to work on my craft. My wife, Maria, was still in college and she'd hang out with me in my office late into the night. After she would finish her homework, she would curl up on my couch and we would talk about our future together. This was when we first talked of our shared dream of running a design agency. We also spoke about marriage, children, travel, and how we were going to reach those goals. One thing on that future list was to write a book. I had just read *Paul Rand* by Steven Heller and was blown away, not only by Paul's work and story, but also by his legacy. He helped define the rules for brand identity design in a world and culture that didn't have many rules. I remember looking at the cover of that book and imagining how it would feel to see my name on a similar design book.

Over the next twenty years, I knuckled down and put in long hours at boutique design studios, a huge marketing firm, a global advertising agency, and in-house for a top ten brand. I studied how each company ran and how they tackled brand identity design. Then I took everything I learned and applied it to running Peters Design Company with Maria.

For years, I've received messages from people around the world asking me if I had a book that explained how I design brand identity systems. Maria finally told me, "Allan, you need to make it known that you want to write a book and the publishers will find you." So, I did. I created a video review of two design books and at the end I said that I was reading them as research for a book I would like to write. Jonathan Simcosky from Rockport watched the entire 20-minute video, heard my admission, and sent me an email saying he wanted to make my dream a reality.

You are currently holding that book in your hands. On the following 200+ pages I will teach you how I do what I do. I will share the exact logo development process that I use with each of my clients at Peters Design Company and show an array of real-life case studies so that you can see this unique method in action. By the end of our time together you will be personally acquainted with the Peters Design Company process of designing a brand identity system that will last for generations.

The Pursuit of Perfection

The Eames Lounger was designed in 1956, and is still widely considered the epitome of modern design. It is a simple, beautiful, and comfortable bent-plywood design that tells a story. It has a timeless design that cannot be improved upon. It is perfect. There has been no reason to make any revisions because Ray and Charles Eames got it right. They were able to accomplish this goal by spending years perfecting their craft and studying the great designers that came before them.

I feel that a great logo should be approached in a similar manner. A logo should not need to be revised every ten years simply because it goes out of style. My career has been devoted to creating marks that are not trend driven. They are equally simple, unique, and memorable while standing the test of time. The way I achieve this is with hard work, research, strategy, craftsmanship, and a love of learning.

Why should you trust me? Good question. Like all designers, I started at the beginning with no idea what I was doing. I was just a kid who loved to draw and that love has fueled my creativity for the past 43 years. As I grew older, my love of drawing grew stronger. As that passion swelled, my skills also leveled up. I have had the opportunity to design multiple billion-dollar brands, have been fortunate enough to win many major awards for design, and have happily had the opportunity to speak about design in such places as Facebook, Disney, and the AIGA National conference.

More importantly, I absolutely love logo design. I think about it in the shower, on walks, while driving or biking. I sometimes even design logos in my dreams. No joke. I love what I do for a living. The feeling I get when solving a creative problem or coming up with the perfect solution for a logo is incredibly satisfying. It drives me to be the best designer I am capable of being.

Have you ever met someone who later in life only listens to music from their teens or twenties and is not interested in new music? That mentality can easily happen in the design field. A designer can create a great logo that wins a bunch of awards and then feel like they have reached the pinnacle of their career. After that, they quit trying and lean on that one award for the rest of their career as the crown jewel of their portfolio. That is not the way I work. For me, logo design is all about the pursuit of perfection, and pursuing perfection means attempting to make every project my best project. There's no such thing as the perfect logo, but the passion involved in chasing the perfect logo is what you need to harness to make one that stands the test of time. There is always room to learn and to improve your craft. You only need to be open to it.

To be clear, this book will not teach you drive and passion. You need to bring those to the table if you want to succeed. Everything else can be taught. I can teach you all about the art, the theory, and the process to design an iconic logo, but you need to work hard and you need to love what you do. You can't cut corners. My process is not an easy one, but if you dig deep, you will find gold.

Do you have that level of passion and drive? If so, then buckle up. I am going to help you push your craft to the next level. I'm going to teach you everything I have spent years learning, and will not hold anything back. I want you to be amazing. That is why I wrote this book for you.

The Beginning

As an artist, input directly impacts output. Your story matters. The way you were raised, the trials you faced, and the battles you have won define character. Your character plays a role in your decision making when working with clients, running a business, or deciding how much effort to put into a project. So that is why I thought it would be helpful to share my story with you.

I started at the beginning with nothing more than an interest in drawing. I can remember the exact moment that I fell in love with art. I was six years old and my mother was driving me to McRea Park for a comic drawing class. At the time, I only drew the typical stick figure, sunshine, and clouds drawings that most kids begin with. I was mostly excited to spend the afternoon with my buddy Mychal Herron. Mychal was a quiet kid like me, so we usually played silently side by side and were very happy not having to deal with extroverts while we were together. When we got to our class, I stared blankly at my white paper while I waited for the class to start. Mychal began to draw spaceships. Really cool-looking spaceships made from only triangles. Easy, right? Anyone can draw a triangle. I loved spaceships. I studied his technique and learned from him.

I began filling blank pages with triangular space battles. Over the next few weeks, whenever I'd go over to Mychal's house, I would bust out the paper and pencils and ask him to draw with me.

For the rest of my childhood, I was obsessed with drawing. I filled my school notebook margins and drew on the desks. I would even skip my high school science and history classes so that I could sneak over to the art room.

At the College of Visual Arts (CVA), I learned print making, photography, drawing, painting, illustration, sculpture, and my favorite—graphic design. When I found graphic design, I fell in love. It was what I was made for. A blend of geometry, problem solving, and art. It would be a career where I could draw every day while helping people using my gifts.

I made it a point to take all of the design-related classes that CVA offered. Filling my schedule with any class I could find related to design, such as illustration, color theory, and photography, all with the intention of strengthening my skill set as a designer.

In the early stages as a designer, you learn so much so quickly. You are developing not only your technical skills, but also your level of taste. My goal was to become a designer and I was going to do whatever it took to achieve that goal. I spent my senior year

Top:
School Photo
1988

Middle:
Triangle Spaceship
1985

Bottom:
High School Drawing
1997

Next Spread Top:
College Drawing
2000

Next Spread Middle:
Matt's Birth
Announcement Sketch
2010

Next Spread Bottom:
On Set
2012

redesigning every piece of my design portfolio with fresh eyes. I did this on top of my other classes and assignments. I knew that in the end, what mattered was not my degree or my grades, but instead my portfolio and my attitude. I slept very little that year. I would be up until midnight most nights refining and redesigning my work to perfect it. I developed a work ethic that was like an unstoppable tank.

When I graduated from CVA in 2003 the economy was tanking. Most design firms were losing clients and laying off employees. It was not the ideal economic climate in which to be searching for your first job. I had friends who had over 30 interviews with no bites. I landed my first interview at a small design studio called Initio. I presented my refined portfolio with as much heart as I could. I offered to work late hours, clean the production room, and do any menial tasks that no one else was willing to take on. I pretty much begged for the job. And I got it. I started as an intern and worked late almost every night, not because they asked, and not because I needed to, but because I wanted to prove that I was not just intern material, I was indispensable.

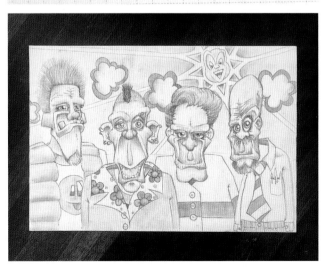

While working at Initio, I met my future wife and business partner, Maria. She was in college studying interior design, creative writing, and marketing. Most nights she would come hang out on the couch in my office to do her homework while I worked late into the night. When she finished her work, we would talk about our hopes and dreams for the future. One of them was to start a design agency together so that we could collaborate and build each other up.

After Initio, I worked for Luis Fitch at Uno and learned about color and culture. I was there for only three months, but to this day I use bits of knowledge that I learned from Luis.

Next, I worked at a small studio called Industrio, where I was brought in as the senior designer. My boss, EJ McNulty, trusted me completely and let me take the reins on the design while he focused on selling the work through. With so much creative freedom, I was able to develop my personal style. I also had the opportunity to watch how a small agency functioned, learning about contracts, paperwork, billing, and attracting new business.

Most of our clients at Industrio were in the outdoor recreational field. We had boat clients, ATV trailer clients, and fishing clients. While developing a new brand identity for our client Frabill, which has an ice fishing focus, we were on an undisclosed lake with a handful of professional ice fishermen shooting images for a catalog and print campaign. As the art director, one of my jobs was to sketch out the day's shoot. There was no time built in to scout the lake, so I left each morning before the sun rose. I was to hop on a snowmobile (which I had never

driven before) and drive around the lake stopping to make marks on a printed map and to sketch out my shots for the day. Knowing that I didn't have much time, and because it was well below zero degrees, I wanted to do the job quickly.

I took off on the snowmobile going around 80 mph. Most people would probably not suggest driving a snowmobile around a lake in the dark going 80 mph, but I figured, what could I possibly hit?! Twenty minutes into my assignment, I started hitting small bumps of snow that the wind had created. I was getting a half foot of air off each one and thought it was pretty cool and that I was getting the hang of this whole snowmobile thing. A few seconds later, I went off a bump that was at least three feet high. I was airborne for what felt like five minutes. When I landed, I immediately dropped my speed and took it nice and slow. Long story short, I got my scouting done before breakfast and we had a killer shoot. I learned a ton about directing a photo shoot and about snowmobiling in the dark.

Next, I took a job at an advertising agency as a senior art director. This is a completely different field from pure design. I still designed brand identity projects when the agency picked them up, but the majority of my work was ad campaigns. When I got the job, the first thing I did was to buy a book on advertising and read it tip-to-tail. Up to that point, I had only created one broadcast spot and it had a budget of only $5,000. Now that I was in the big leagues, I needed to know what I was doing. Learning a new trade was valuable for my development as a well-rounded creative professional. I learned to work in harmony with a copywriter. Not only on the words, but sharing in the ideation process. I also learned a lot about how to sell work. No one can sell work better than an art director.

My last job working for a boss was at Target. I was about to combine everything I had learned so far and use that knowledge on a huge brand. I designed brand identities, art directed photo shoots, created in-store marketing, designed event materials, and created all forms of advertising, including broadcast. It was a great experience and I was able to see how a successful brand functioned from the inside. Working in-house differed from a traditional agency role in that it allowed me to be honest with clients when they were making a poor decision and it gave me the freedom to pitch new project ideas.

But the most valuable lesson I learned at Target was that I worked best and most efficiently when on my own. My time was not eaten up by meetings, arguments, team-building events, check-ins about check-ins, and "how was your weekend" conversations. When I worked from home or on the bus, I could fly through projects. My experience at an ad agency had taught me to be ultra-efficient with my time. I began taking on freelance projects that I would tackle on the bus to and from work. My last year at Target, I made more money on my eight hours of weekly commuting than I did in my 40-hour-a-week day job. It was time for Maria and me to follow our dream of starting Peters Design Company.

Peters Design Company

In 2008, we started Peters Design Company. In 2015, I quit my day job to work full-time at PDCo. I was all in and could finally use my gifts to help companies that shared our views and beliefs.

In the past seven years, we have branded eight churches and three cities and have done more passion projects than I can count on my fingers and toes. It's changed how I work. I have applied everything I have learned in my career to guiding our clients and successfully running our business.

One of the greatest assets of running our own agency without employees and simultaneously home schooling our children is that we are not tethered to any one location. We have spent the winter down on the Gulf Coast multiple times while still running the business at full steam. It makes our lifestyle so much more flexible.

These days, I focus and get my work done for the week between Monday and Thursday and take Friday through Sunday off to enjoy life with my family. I am so thankful to be alive and be blessed with this beautiful family and business.

Chapter 1
What Makes a
Logo Last?

When looking back on the past, there are certain logos that you remember. The CBS Eye, The Apple, The Shell, The Swoosh, and The Peacock. These are just a few examples off the top of my head, but I am sure you have a handful of favorites as well.

What makes these marks so special? How do they still feel modern after decades of use? Why have they not been changed or refined? I have devoted my career to exploring this topic. Spending countless hours scouring antique stores, small-town museums, and thrift stores looking for inspiration. All in the pursuit of a formula that I can apply to the projects that I design for my clients. As they say, the proof is in the pudding. What I mean is, when you start making logos that achieve this long-lasting appeal, people will let you know. You hear it from your clients, social comments, emails, and DMs. People are going to let you know that you are creating iconic marks that will stand the test of time.

I have narrowed the long-lasting logo formula down to three things you cannot control and seven things that you can. It is important to remember, you cannot control the timeline, you cannot control the marketing budget, and you cannot control the product quality. However, what you can control is your personal passion, the visual beauty, the originality, the functionality, the color, the memorability, and the simplicity of the mark. All ten of these pillars need to be addressed to successfully create a mark that will stand the test of time. In this chapter, I will walk you through each of these pillars individually. By digging into each, you will come to understand my thinking and be able to apply it to your own work.

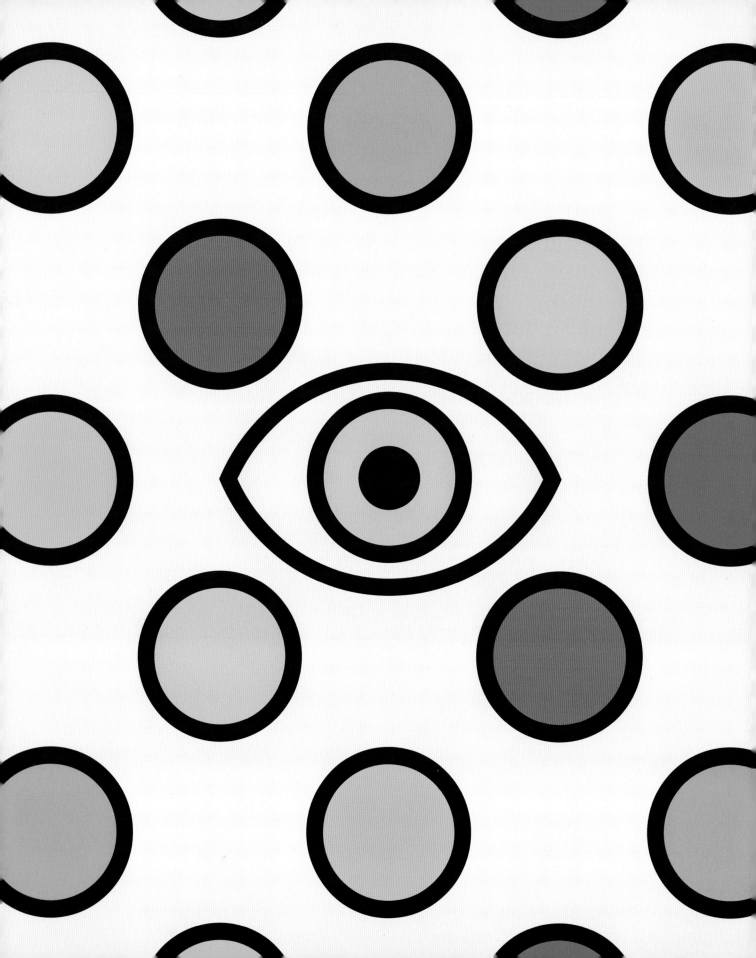

Time

The true test of a long-lasting mark is time. Over time, a trend-driven or poorly crafted logo will show its age. It will be replaced with a mark that hopefully solves the obvious issues that arise. On the other hand, a strategically pure and well-crafted mark will grow stronger over time. With each meeting the logo will become more and more embedded in the viewers' long-term memory. This is key. When a mark is embedded in enough of your audience's long-term memories, you will not need to use words anymore. The brand mark can stand on its own without typography.

Unless you have a DeLorean decked out with a flux capacitor, time is one of the three pillars that we have no control over as designers. I think it's still an important pillar to understand so that you can explain to a client why a mark does not feel iconic right out of the gate. I can guarantee you that the Nike Swoosh was not as impactful when it was designed in 1971 as it is now 50 years later. Time is a powerful ally if you have successfully navigated the other nine long-lasting logo pillars.

The Marketing Budget

The first time you drive somewhere, it feels like time stretches to the horizon. You are aware of every turn. You notice obscure landmarks and the mystery of it all keeps you focused on every little detail. The drive home feels like it takes much less time. When you return to that location over your lifetime, your brain can drive there on autopilot while you chat with a friend or listen to a podcast. The repetition of the same drive has been written to your long-term memory.

In the same way, for a mark to become truly iconic it needs repeat viewings. To make sure people are seeing the mark, a strong and consistent marketing budget is required. If McDonald's only had one location in a small town and did no advertising, the logo would not be nearly as iconic as it is. It has become iconic partly based on repeat viewings achieved by a large marketing budget. Billboards, print ads, roadside signs, and even the architecture itself feature elements of the brand mark. Repeated viewings drive the mark into the long-term memory of the viewer. That is what you want.

As a designer, you unfortunately do not have control over the marketing budget. The only control you have is deciding whether to accept a project from a potential client. Obviously, you can try to choose clients with traditionally larger marketing budgets. Getting lucky with a start-up is a real gamble if you are hoping to have your logo design seen by a huge audience. However, with a start-up you will have much more flexibility with subject matter and style. There is nothing set in stone with a start-up. I personally try to keep a balance of start-ups and larger established clients with the hope of getting the best of both worlds.

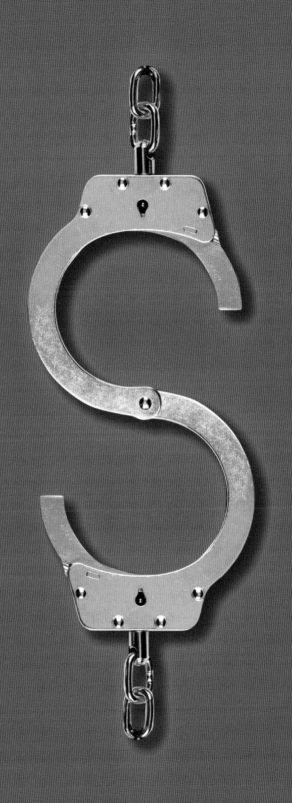

Product Quality

When starting a new business, it is important to have a good product. Companies with big budgets tend to do market research in advance to make sure that the product they plan to bring to market is going to sell well. Unfortunately, start-ups do not usually have the budget for market research and user testing. To be honest, many of my clients have a difficult time scraping up the money for a quality brand identity. Unfortunately, it does not matter how good the brand identity turns out if your client has a bad product. It's destined to fail.

As designers, we do not have control over the quality of our client's products. What we do have control over is which clients we take on. Not all designers have the luxury of picking and choosing clients, and that's OK. Sometimes a designer just needs the money. Other times they might be working for an agency that is picking the clients. Either way, do not feel bad if it feels like you are designing a logo and color system for the Titanic. Life goes on and there will be more clients. My best advice is to be honest with your client about their product. Perhaps there is a simple innovative solution that will improve their product. If you are able to save a client from failing, they will definitely trust you with more work and more responsibility in the future.

Personal Passion

The majority of little kids love to make art. They are passionate about it. As they grow older, many lose that passion and they only make art when it is required at school. They rush through the assignment and move on. Few children make it to adulthood with the same level of passion for creativity as they did when they were six.

Keeping this love of art alive in your life is imperative to becoming a talented designer. Once design students become professionals, their job can become their passion and their lives fill with other interests like family and hobbies. However, you must keep that same six-year-old level of enthusiasm for making art alive in your heart.

When you are passionate about creating art, you push to make your work brilliant and you have a fun time creating it. That fire bleeds through and shows in the work. Clients see it. The target audience sees it. Everyone sees it and they all want to be a part of it.

All long-lasting logos are clearly and undeniably a labor of love. When people see that passion, they cannot help but fall in love.

Universal Beauty

We have all been told that beauty is in the eye of the beholder; however, I believe that there is a universal level of taste that is appreciated by the masses. As designers learn in our art school educations, there are certain tenets of design that tend to create visually appealing compositions. Certain artwork is viewed as universally beautiful by the majority of people. Take the painting *Starry Night* by Vincent van Gogh as an example. Not everyone thinks it is beautiful, but most people do. Van Gogh marries visual interest, color harmony, storytelling, and a looping composition into the artwork.

All iconic, time-honored classic marks are universally beautiful. The beauty of a mark can come through in a variety of ways. Sometimes it's the perfect level of visual balance between the positive and negative space. Other times it's the rhythm between the linework. And at other times it is the perfect balance of simplicity and storytelling. No matter which design principle makes a logo visually appealing, they are all widely considered beautiful.

One way that I test a logo to ensure that it is universally beautiful is to mock up a potential brand mark on a hat. I then ask the client if they would be proud to wear this hat. If a logo is aesthetically pleasing, they should want to wear it as an accessory. There are many logos in the world that are clever, but you would never be caught dead wearing them.

As a designer, it is easy to think that all of your work is beautiful. The way to identify universal beauty is by having a group of people react to your work. With the advent of social media, it is easy to quickly find out which pieces of your work people gravitate toward or what they "like" best. Use that data to help guide the development of your visual aesthetic. This process can lead to an iconic visual style that people will know you for.

Originality

Logos need to be simple so that they are functional. However, if they are too simple, there is a good chance that they are not original. There is an abundance of companies in the world with a simple shape like a circle or a square for a logo. They can all fight about who had the circle or square first, but none of them are memorable because they are the same.

Remember when we talked earlier about wanting your audience to remember the brand and develop an affinity for it? That is impossible to achieve if the logo is not unique. When your logo is trite, then your audience will believe that everything else about the brand is cliché.

It is important to find the perfect balance point between simplicity and originality. The best way to do this is to explore marks that you believe achieve this feat and then study their level of complexity to see what works best. If you can come up with an extremely simple and trademarkable brand mark, then I applaud you.

When you finish a design, be sure to search the internet to see if it has been designed before. You can search Google with images as well as search key words on Behance and Dribbble. In addition, a professional trademark search is always recommended.

Functionality

A well-designed logo is functional. For a logo to be adequately used by a client it needs to be simple. Simple enough to work as a favicon at 16x16 pixels. Simple enough that it can be embroidered at small sizes or stamped into concrete, if needed. The functionality requirements are going to shift depending on the company. However, it is important that you future-proof the logo for any use that may arise.

One thing I have noticed in marks that have survived over 50 years is that they are as simple and functional as any mark designed today. When Raymond Loewy was designing the Shell logo, he had no idea that it would need to be functional in social avatars, on mobile phones, or as a favicon. But he made it simple enough that it has passed the test of time. There has been no reason to update his design for Shell. It is the perfect balance of functionality and visual style.

When you feel that a design is finished, do some tests on it. Try it out at tiny sizes and see how it looks. Is it still identifiable? If your client has the budget, try embroidering it at a few sizes. How small can you make it before the logo loses recognizability? You will quickly know if the logo is too complex. In the City of Eagan project that you will see in the Case Studies chapter, we did this exact test because it was important that city staff be able to wear embroidered clothing as part of their jobs.

If you find that your design has issues, identify the places where it first breaks down visually. Overly thin lines and tight negative space tend to be the major issues I see in logo designs in small-scale applications. At other times the issue is that the mark is too complex. Once you have identified the pain points, go back and figure out ways to solve them. Thicker lines? More negative space between each element? Is there any way to make the entire design simpler without losing the meaning behind the mark?

Color Palette

Strategically, color serves two main purposes. The first purpose is to help communicate the story that the logo is telling. A logo of a tree will usually be green for this exact reason. The second purpose is to stand out from the competition.

To stand out from the competitors, it is smart to do a competitive analysis of all competing brands prior to picking a color. The new brand should not be the same color as its competitors' if you want it to have a distinct impact. Another way to do this is by using saturated colors so that the logo stands out when placed side by side with a competitor. It's all about leading the consumer's eye toward your brand.

I have found that most brand marks that last for 50 years tend toward fully saturated colors. The two most common logo colors are red and blue. That does not mean they are better colors; it is simply that they are commonly used. In my experience, there is not one single color that specifically stands out. Explore the entire color wheel and see what works. I personally aim for bright and pure hues as well as warm tones.

When I was in college, one of my painting teachers taught me to never choose a pure black or a pure white unless I had a good reason. She said to warm up or cool down my blacks and whites to work in harmony with the rest of my color palette. I've applied this rationale to all the color palettes in my design work. I think it helps to tie a palette together and it creates visual harmony with your colors.

Keep an eye out for great color palettes from the past and present. When you discover a palette that makes you smile, study it and learn from it. Figure out why those colors feel good when paired. The color palettes that draw your eye will help you begin to develop an overall color style. Your passion for color will be reflected in the work you create.

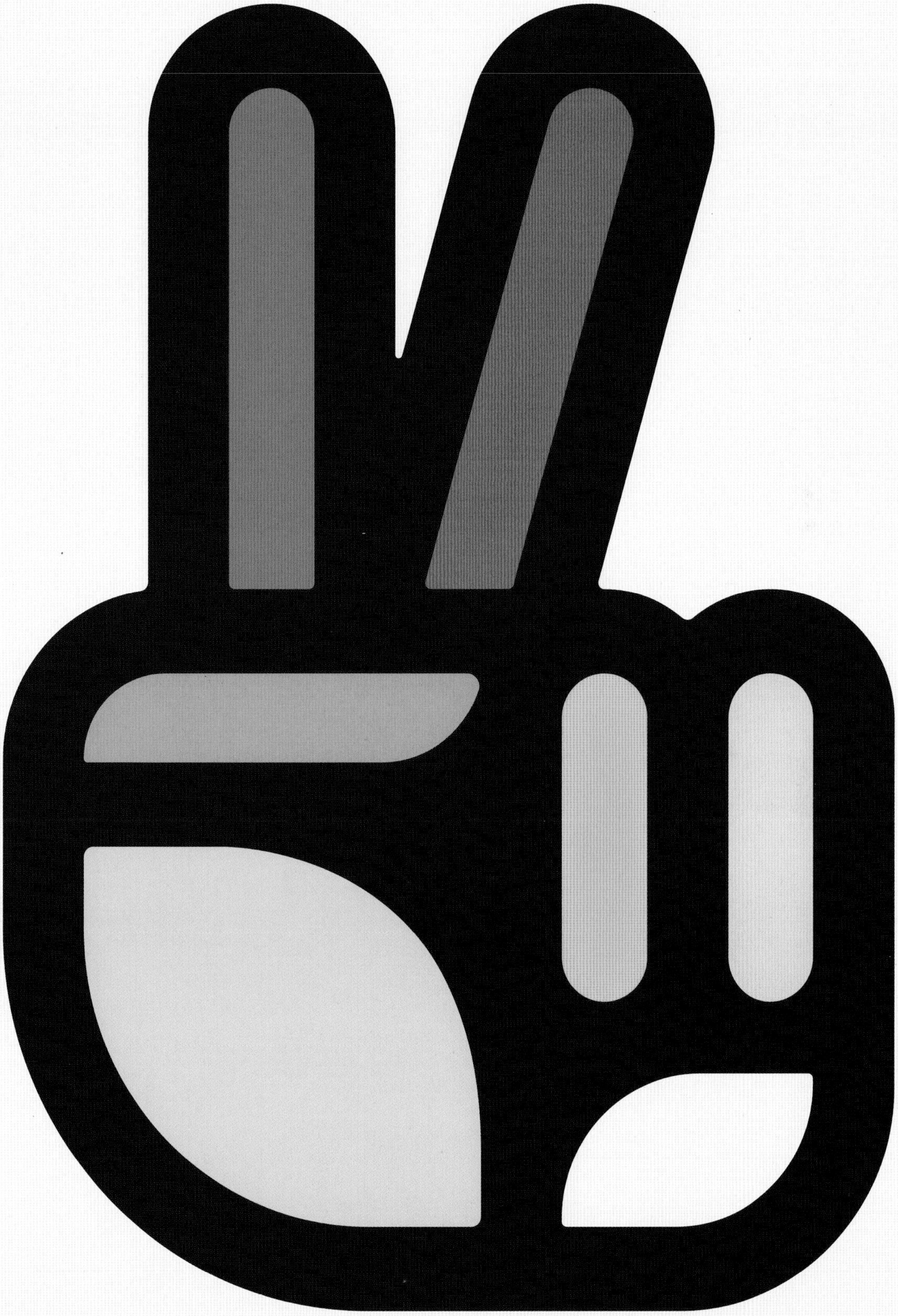

Story

One of the signs of a classic brand mark is memorability. One of the greatest ways to make a brand mark memorable is to infuse it with a story. The Nike Swoosh is a story about speed. That's all you need: a hook to remember.

What if you met two boys, one named Bob and another named Hawk. After the introduction, they left, and you never saw them again. A day later someone asks you what their names were. Whose name are you going to remember easier? Hawk's of course. It is unique and it has a story. The same goes for logos. If you add a simple story to the visual representation of a brand mark, it will make it into the viewers' long-term memory with fewer repeat viewings.

Abstract logos can be visually memorable as well. Perhaps the mark uses a unique optical effect or negative and positive space is used in a memorable way. What you want to avoid is uninspired logos that are so simple that there is no reason to remember them. Examples of this are plain geometric shapes or generic letterforms. There is nothing more forgettable than a letter in a circle.

Simplicity

To be functional, a logo needs to be simple. The trick with simplicity is to be as uncomplicated as possible without losing the story, the originality, or the beauty.

When designing a logo, I first like to capture my idea in a sketch. I then take it onto the computer to vectorize it. After that, I start to explore the level of simplicity. I start removing elements. I take away as many elements as possible until the logo stops communicating the intended message. Finding that tipping point is key when creating a logo that lasts.

Make sure that the logo's simplicity does not subtract from its memorability. As you make a design more and more simple, it should strengthen the concept and it will become purer. If simplifying your idea makes the idea weaker or less memorable, you will know that you went too far. Spend time experimenting with the simplicity of your design. You will probably be surprised at how uncomplicated you can make the logo without sacrificing its impact.

Chapter 2
Brand Mark Process

Having a clear and deliberate process is incredibly important when designing logos. First of all, it helps an uneducated client understand why it costs thousands of dollars and takes about six weeks to design a logo. Also, it gives you and your client a clear road map so that if your client goes out of scope with additional rounds of ideation or revision, you can be compensated for the additional work.

In this chapter I will share my exact logo design process. It is different from that of any other designer or agency that I have come across. It's based on everything I have learned in school, working at design shops, and reading books. Over my 20-year career I have tried many different processes, refining and distilling my experience into what I am about to share with you. For me, this process works like a well-oiled machine. It runs perfectly. To be honest, it is not the easiest process. In fact, it is demanding. Due to that, my logos cost more to allow for the project to run a full six weeks, but the results are amazing.

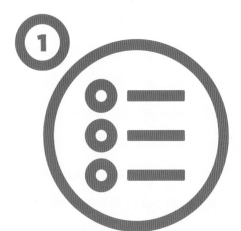

Brand Noun Process

The first step is to define what subject matter you and the client think is strategically appropriate for the brand mark.

Sketch Phase

Using the approved brand nouns begin to create rough sketches. Quantity is more important than quality. Focus on the ideas, not the details.

Combining Brand Nouns

By finding interesting combinations of approved brand nouns, you can create unique and ownable brand marks.

Vectorizing & Gridding

Take your rough sketches and bring them to life using geometry, simple shapes, and a grid structure.

Brand Mark Exploration

Begin to refine your marks and make them perfect. Only develop your top ideas.

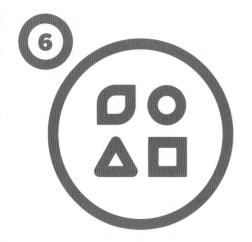

Brand System

Take your top three brand marks and develop them into full brand systems. This includes horizontal and vertical logos as well as badges. Use your approved brand mark to guide your choices both typographically and geometrically.

Brand Noun Process

I start every client logo project with a brand noun process. The point of this exercise is to figure out the subject matter of the brand mark. I begin by coming up with a list of nouns (person, place, or thing) that could be the subject matter of the symbol. If you have an idea that you feel needs to be represented but is not a noun, you need to come up with a noun that serves as a metaphor for that word.

For example, let's say you are designing a logo for a bank and you want to represent the word "trust." What you can do is a quick Google image search for "trust icons." See what comes up. It will probably be images like a shield, a key, a keyhole, shaking hands, or a lock. If any of that subject matter seems appropriate, add it to your noun list.

If you are stuck on where to start or you feel that you do not know the brand well enough, ask your client to tell you all about their company and their core values. If they have an existing website or brochure, read it and get to know them. This will make the process smoother.

Once I have a solid list of 15 to 25 brand nouns that I know will be easy to work with and represent the brand well, I send the list to my client and I walk them through the brand noun process, making sure to explain in detail the definition of a noun and how to deal with any non-noun words that arise. You would be amazed how many clients send me brand noun lists that are less than half nouns. Clearly explaining this process will save you time and will keep you from having to explain to your client that they did the exercise wrong.

Including the client in this process is absolutely paramount. No one knows a brand better than someone working on it day in and day out. It also includes them in the strategy and helps them truly collaborate early on in a way that's strategically impactful.

Once I have explained the brand noun process, I give my clients a homework assignment. I ask that each of the people on the client side who will be an approver of the final logo come up with a brand noun list of their own. Once I have everyone's lists compiled, I organize them by category, removing all of the doubles. Then I schedule a meeting with my client to help them narrow down the list to about 15 brand nouns that I will use to inspire my initial sketches.

Narrowing down the list is more important than making the list. It eliminates everything that the client does not want to see. That way when you are selling logo ideas in the later stages of the project, the decision will only be based on the aesthetics of the design and not the subject matter.

Hardin Valley
Brand Nouns

1. Sunshine
2. Hills
3. Valley
4. Rivers
5. Heart
6. Praying Hands
7. Hands
8. Open Hands
9. Corner Stone
10. Connected Lines
11. Connected Shapes
12. Home
13. Infinity
14. Tree
15. Leaf

Fifty Sketches

Do not skip the sketch phase. Do not rush the sketch phase. Embrace and enjoy the sketch phase. This is where the real magic happens. This is the fun part.

Have you ever heard the saying "You can't polish a turd"? It means that if you do not have a good idea to begin with, you will be wasting your time refining it.

Inexperienced designers tend to take their first idea or two directly into the final phase of design, where it is digitized and finalized. I have witnessed many designers spend a week "polishing" a mediocre logo. They should have spent that precious time focused on idea generation.

Finding a good idea is like fishing. The more times you cast your lure, the better chance you have of catching fish. The more fish you catch, the better chance you have of catching a trophy-sized fish. This same logic applies with logo design. The more sketches you draw, the better chance you have of striking gold with a brilliant idea.

I like to jump into the creative process with a goal. I create a minimum of 50 rough sketches. The quality of the sketches should be rough, just detailed enough to capture the idea. Refining a sketch at this phase is a waste of time. Quantity is king. Save your refinement time for only the best ideas.

Combining Brand Nouns

The sketch phase is more than just drawing logos. It is all about creating a huge quantity of unique ideas. And one of the best ways to do this is to combine multiple brand nouns together. This is easier said than done. A shield as a logo seems not only unoriginal, but also cliché. A lightning bolt on its own is not at all clever or exciting. However, when you combine a shield and a lightning bolt into one icon, suddenly you have something unique and clever. There are many ways to visually combine brand nouns. You can use negative space, overlapping geometry, visual rhythm, visual flow, or even an unexpected twist. In this section, I will break down each of these methods and give examples to help you achieve each one. These methods should get you to fifty sketches quickly. They will also help you begin to think about logo design in a whole new light.

Overlapping Geometry

One of the ways I combine subject matter when I design brand marks is by using a technique called "overlapping geometry." I start by quickly making a pencil sketch of the brand nouns that I would like to combine. In this case a leaf, a sun, and a water droplet. Next I draw as many simple leaves, suns, and drops as I can think of until I have a page filled with basic icons. After that, I go through each sketch and draw the geometric skeleton of each. I examine the icons for geometric overlap in their grid structure. Can the curve of a droplet double as the vein of a leaf? Perhaps a rising sun could be used to complete the curved edge of a leaf? Sometimes I make a discovery that makes me laugh out loud at how awesome it is. The best combinations feel like they belong together. You don't have to work hard to combine them. This is one of my favorite techniques.

Right:
Firecraft Pizza
2015

Golden Bear
2021

Freadom
2015

Jet Financial
2010

Negative Space Logos

When creating the mark for Firecraft Pizza, I combined a flame and a pizza slice using negative space. A flame or a pizza slice on its own is not memorable because of all of the pre-existing flame logos and pizza logos. Creating an original and ownable flame or pizza could leave you with an overly complex and difficult-to-use brand mark. The great thing about combining these two elements into one cohesive negative space logo is that it's simple, ownable, and it tells a visual story that is memorable.

This mark uses the negative space of the flame to define the outer edge of the pizza slice. I created it by finding the visual overlap between the two icons. However, not all brand nouns can be combined to create visual harmony. Actually, it is quite rare.

I am going to teach you the trick that I use to find the visual overlap. First, take a sketch pad and draw rough sketches of all of the different ways you could design an icon for a pizza slice. Next, do the same exploration for flame icons. Now look at your page of sketches. Scan the flame and pizza icons that you've created. Do you see any similar shapes? Does the triangle of a pizza slice find its way into the geometry of a flame icon? Could it? How about a circular pizza? Is there overlap between that and one of the flame icon sketches? Keep looking and trying out a variety of combinations to see if they work. Sometimes you will strike gold.

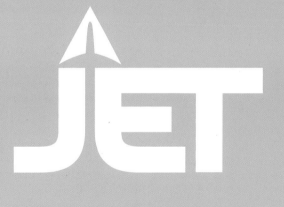

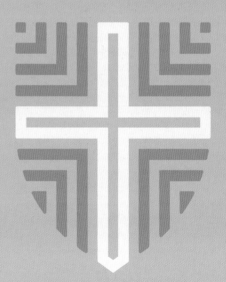

Left:
PDCo Type Fight P
2015

PDCo Transparency
2015

PDCo Daydream Brewery
2018

PDCo Armor of God
2017

Visual Rhythm

Having a strong visual rhythm between positive and negative space can help to tie two brand nouns together. In the Armor of God brand mark pictured here, I have combined a cross and a shield. By adding evenly spaced lines running around the cross, it not only helps transition the geometry from one to the other, but it also draws your eye into the center of the mark and creates visual energy.

Be careful, because this technique can be overdone. Make sure that the final mark is still simple. If you can shave off a few of the lines while still keeping the same idea, then shave them off. Remember that you are making a logo, not an illustration.

This can be a difficult technique to master; however, with practice you will get a feel for it and know when it feels right.

Right:
Texas Wine Club
2022

PDCo Stay Home. Stay Safe.
2020

PDCo Justice & Peace
2020

Love of Learning
2013

An Unexpected Twist

One of the great things about combining two brand nouns is that you end up with something fresh and interesting even if the subject matter on its own might feel expected or boring. A good example is the Love of Learning illustration that I created for Inch X Inch.

An apple on its own would feel like a knock off of Apple computers. A heart on its own can be boring or expected. However, when combined they can become fresh and unexpected. This makes it more memorable and ownable. When narrowing down the brand noun list with your client, be sure they understand this. Without proper guidance, it's all too easy to remove the brand nouns that feel like well-trodden ground. You do not want to lose amazing subject matter because your client feels you will not be able to transform it into something original.

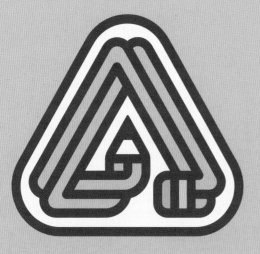

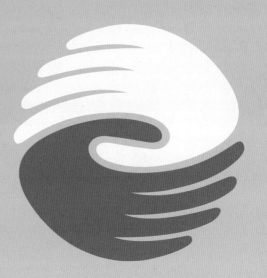

Left:
PDCo Creativity
2016

PDCo Transparency
2015

City of Shoreview
2017

PDCo Hand in Hand
2011

Visual Flow

Visual flow is created by using the linework of a brand mark to direct the viewer's eye to the center of the mark. The City of Shoreview's brand mark on the facing page is a great example of this. The waves lead you from the bottom of the mark toward the trees, and the negative space of the trees leads your eye down to the water. Every element is pulling the eye back in.

This technique of compositional movement was frequently used by master painters of the Renaissance period. The artist would strategically orient their primary subject matter along with specific colors within their compositions so that the viewer's eyes would flow intentionally throughout the painting. I will tell you right now, that if this technique has worked successfully since the 1300s, it is a solid design principle.

When reviewing your brand nouns, look for geometry with movement built into it— for example, arrow shapes, chevrons, and any other visual iconography that conveys energy. Try combining these in ways where all of the visual energy converges in the center of the mark.

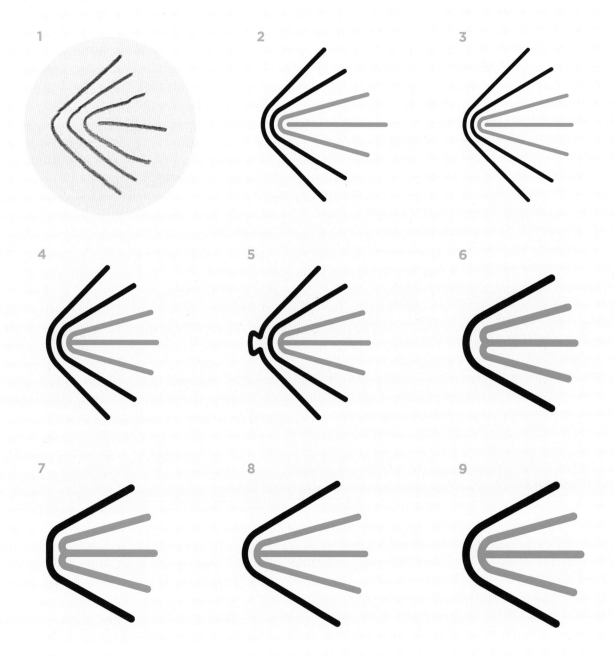

Vectorizing & Gridding

Here is where you bring the polish. Once I have selected 15 sketches that I am very happy with, I take them into Adobe Illustrator and begin the vectorization process. I build out geometric rules to keep the elements as simple as possible.

For instance, I like to make sure everything works at small sizes, so I prefer to make my line weight thick. That said, if the lines are too thick, you have to account for your lack of negative space. The negative space in a brand mark is just as important as the positive space.

At this point I try many variations of the sketch. I will try different angles, different weights, different amounts of lines or design elements. With each move, I am trying to shave off just a bit of complexity to see how simple I can make the mark without losing the idea. How can I communicate the sketch in the fewest number of moves?

Remember that you have an unlimited amount of space in an illustrator document. As you design alternate variations of the idea, continue to save the versions that show promise. When you have all of the versions that you like finished, put them side by side to see which one works the best. Be sure to try them at small sizes, in both black on white and white on black.

Once I have my final deck prepared, I go back through the options to determine the five weakest marks. I then jump back into my sketchbook to see if I can replace them with something better.

The First-Round Brand Mark Presentation

My goal for the brand mark presentation is to show all 15 brand mark options in black and white. At this stage I do not show any typography or color, just the symbols.

I start my presentation with a recap of the approved brand nouns. With each idea, I show it in black on white and white on black. I also list the brand nouns that are referenced in each logo so that when the client looks at the PDF when I'm not there they remember what we talked about.

After talking through each of the 15 brand marks individually, I finish the deck with all 15 options on one slide so that we can compare them easily and discuss the merits of each. It's important to take the lead in the presentation and act as a guide. You should have your top three directions chosen and placed strategically in the deck so that they make the most impact.

Yes, your work should speak for itself, but I do strongly suggest presenting this phase instead of sending a PDF in an email. That way you can answer questions and fend off bad feedback on the fly. This is the most crucial presentation and you need to defend the integrity of the work. Remember that you are the expert. That is why you were hired to do the job.

Educating your client on the tenets of design is a big part of your job. The goal of this meeting is to have your client pick their top three brand marks. Make sure that they know the goal of the meeting before you start the presentation.

My last tip is to keep the meeting and conversation positive and constructive. Explain before you discuss the final logos that the client should not point out the brand marks they dislike, but instead focus on what they do like.

When I am working with a large room of client stakeholders, I will present the first 15 marks individually without client commentary. When we reach the last slide of my deck that shows all 15 options side by side, I will ask everyone in the room to quietly write down on a piece of paper which three they would pick. Then I go around the room and discuss each person's choices while tallying up their votes. This keeps the person in charge on the client end from dominating the conversation and limiting the opinions of the people in the room who rank lower on the corporate totem pole. Also, make sure you start the reveal of people's favorites with your top three picks. All these tips will not only help you make a sale, but also help you sell the best work.

ORIGINAL

REVISION 1

REVISION 2

Revisions & Client Guidance

The key to success in the revision process is understanding the problems that can arise. When a client says, "Make the logo bigger," the problem is that the work is not on-brand. Making the logo bigger will not fix the problem. It will only make it worse. Remember that the client wants the work to be a success. Make sure that you are guiding them on a successful path.

Let's look at this example on the left. The first round of client feedback was to make sure the typography was clearly legible when driving past a water tower on the highway. I could have just picked a different font and moved on, but I looked at this as an opportunity to improve the logo. I solved the problem by creating a custom font that is inspired by the geometry of the brand mark, as shown in Revision 1 of the facing page. The new custom font has some intentionally curved and rounded corners. I also altered the width of the "E" and the "N" so that the "G" would be centered below the icon.

The second round of revision was changing the amount of lines on the hill shape, as the client found them visually overwhelming. There was also a concern that the mark was overly complex for stamped concrete applications. As shown in Revision 2, I easily solved this concern by cropping in tighter on the brand mark and simplifying the hill lines while still clearly communicating that it was a hill.

The result of the revision process can be a stronger mark. The client feedback and partnership on this project helped to make this possible. Be sure to embrace the revision process positively. Never give up on the work.

How to Sell a Strong Mark to a Client

The secret to producing great work is your ability to sell great work. Early in my career, I worked at design agencies where it was part of the culture to fear the client and to do everything they said without question. The work suffered due to the fear of losing the client, when in reality, a strong client partnership can strengthen both the work and the client relationship.

When the client takes control of a project, they take on the role of the creative director. Clients are great at marketing, and creative directors/designers are great at being artists. We really should all stay in our respective roles so that we can solve problems that lead to the best outcomes for everyone—beautiful work that stands the test of time and solves the client's problem.

When I made the transition to working in-house in 2009, I lost my fear of the client because we were on the same team. There was no fear of losing my job or the client. I began to speak up and I took the design wheel. I would be honest with my clients when I felt they were making poor choices that would hurt the work and impact the bottom line. In return, they respected me more and let me take the lead. The work became aesthetically pure and of higher quality. I have taken this same approach when running my own design firm. I always take the lead and guide my clients respectfully through the process.

If you take the back seat, you will not end up where you want to go. Remember you are the expert, the artist, and the specialist. Have confidence and teach your client as you go.

GILBERT

AMERICAN
SCIENCE SERIES
Erector
SET

Chapter 3
Inspiration Hunting

I absolutely love discovering logos of the past that I have never seen before. I find so much inspiration digging in antique stores, estate sales, and small-town museums. If you dig deep enough, you will find inspiring design work created by lesser-known designers of the past. Finding and studying this work makes me a better designer. All of the work that I have created in my lifetime has been inspired by what I discover.

Most modern-day designers never leave their desks. They find their inspiration from other modern-day designers on sites like Pinterest, Dribbble, Behance, and Instagram. When a small pool of modern-day designers only find inspiration in each other, all of their work starts to look the same. You see the same styles used over and over. By deepening your pool of inspiration, the overall work of the masses will become more beautiful and diverse.

Let's be honest. The main reason I love digging for badges, typography, and logos is because it is super fun. The rush you get when you find something truly surprising is thrilling. But there is no need to own all of this stuff. You would end up with a library of dusty junk. All we really need as designers is a good photo.

In this chapter I'm going to take you #badgehunting as I like to call it and we're going to explore some of my favorite honey holes.

What I Look For & Where I Look For It

Location is key when looking at vintage design. Imagine a time before everyone bought everything from Amazon and big-box retailers. Back in the day when you purchased something in Minnesota, chances are it was made in Minnesota. Depending on where you look in the world, you will find a completely different assortment of design work. It is actually fun to take an afternoon when you are on vacation to check out an antique shop in a different part of the world. Chances are you will find all new regional brands that you have never seen before.

When choosing a location to search out treasures I try to avoid big cities. The smaller the town, the less picked through the shops will be. That means you'll find a larger selection of beautiful pieces.

You may ask, why do you waste your days off digging through relics of the past? I'm looking for lost trends and solutions to problems. Logo designers of the past faced many of the same challenges we face today; however they had fewer examples from history to guide them. Much of this stuff was made before guys like Paul Rand and Saul Bass created standards for what a logo should be. It was the wild west of design. Because of that, the solutions tended to be unique and innovative. When I am out #badgehunting I am looking for these specific things: unique badges, bold brand marks, and custom typography.

I am never looking to copy any of this work. Instead, I use it to inspire new ways of looking at my own work. It's a learning tool for me. In a way, by studying the work of the past, I'm being educated by these amazing designers. Like all of the great artists of the past, I am standing on the shoulders of design giants. Wisdom is free and it is out there. You just need to dig a bit.

This is the ORIGINAL *Pabst Blue Ribbon* beer
NATURES CHOICEST PRODUCTS PROVIDE ITS PRIZED FLAVOR
ONLY THE FINEST OF HOPS AND GRAINS ARE USED
Selected as America's Best in 1893

PBR

Pabst
Blue Ribbon
BEER ®

P270 PABST BREWING COMPANY, MILWAUKEE, WIS.

REX
Perpetuum-Elmer

A
R R
L

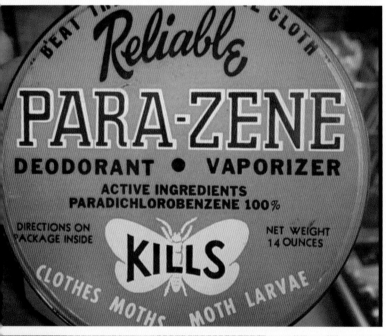

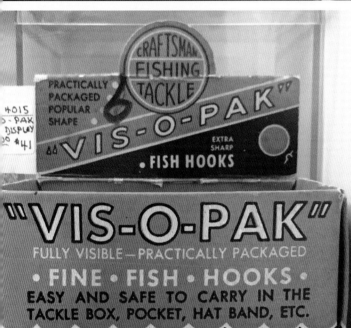

Unique Badges

I try to find badges with interesting shapes or clever ways of dividing up the typographic content. The tendency for modern designers is to just make a circle or an oval, but there are many more unique shapes that can help amplify the story of the brand. Each of these badges has a rich sense of visual storytelling.

ELECTRIC COMPANY

United for Better Service
512 Sibley Street
St. P

Bold Brand Marks

I try to seek out marks that are not trend driven. I love when a mark feels like it could have been designed today when it was actually designed over 50 years ago. I am searching for examples that incorporate the three principles we talked about earlier in the book: simple, unique, and memorable.

Quick Lane

BURLINGTON
NORTHERN
RAILROAD

VESTOCK

fu

AB

Amtrak

MIDLAND

IONEL   BLT 1-76

HOPPE'S

9

Lubricating

Custom Typography

I love to discover unique ways to customize typography. Usually the subtler it is, the more I like it. Currently the trend in logo design is to go as minimal and lifeless as possible. Custom typography is a breath of fresh air. It helps give your design a story, making it more memorable.

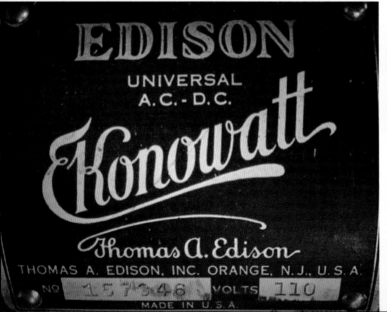

ATLAS

POLISHING

NORTHWESTERN
DRUG COMPANY
MINNEAPOLIS,
U.S.A.

SINCLAIR
PENNANT

CLEANER

QUALITY PLUS
STANLEY
WESTFIELD MASS.

A GUARANTEED PRODUCT

UNION 76

VALVOLINE
The World's First Motor Oil

So Much More

You never know what you are going to find. The key is to just look for good design. Sometimes it is hidden inside a suitcase or on the bottom of a box. You need to dig a bit to find the good stuff. I look for animals, icons, mascots, numbers, pretty much anything that catches my eye. Take a picture and sort out the good stuff later.

MOTOR TUNE-UP TONIC

PERISHABLE KEEP UNDER REFRIGERATION · SILVER SEA · SPICED FISH · NO SPOILAGE GUARANTEE

PACKED BY ALLISON-BEDFORD CO. CHICAGO

DUPONT TYNEX
MADE IN USA
FISHING LINE · MONOFILAMENT
NYLON
MTR. 4,8 KG.
30

ARCO
Products of
AtlanticRichfield

SOUNDESIGN ®
AM Portable Radio
SOUNDESIGN
AM 54 60 70 80 100 120 140 160 KHz
VOLUME
OFF MAX

WINCHESTER ®
UPLAND
PLASTIC SHOTGUN SHELLS
WARNING: KEEP OUT OF THE REACH OF CHILDREN

Sinclair
A GREAT NAME IN OIL

INTERNATIONAL UNION OF FLOUR
GROUND
PACKED
— AND —
UNION HANDLED BY LABEL
BY
UNION
LABOR
AND CEREAL MILL EMPLOYEES.

Chapter 4
Badge Design Process

Many modern design firms will steer you away from creating a badge design. They will tell you that a badge is too complicated and old-fashioned. They are wrong. A great brand system should be modular, including multiple versions of a logo for different media placements, A brand mark for avatars and small spaces. A horizontal logo for compact spaces like a mobile site. A vertical logo for large spaces like signage and T-shirts. That makes sense, right? Then why not a badge for large spaces like murals, packaging, and posters?

A badge is more complex. That is not a bad thing. Telling a more elaborate story makes it more memorable. Badges are not only nostalgic, but can also be very modern depending on how you design them. They are a great tool to add to your brand identity toolbox, especially if you create them properly and intelligently.

In this chapter, I will walk you through external shape creation, shape containers, balancing, and how to create a logo system that includes a badge (or badges). You are not going to find this section in any other logo design book, so buckle up and enjoy something that might open your mind.

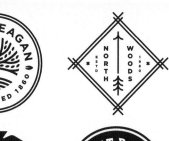

Content Organization

The first step in badge design is to figure out what content you have to work with and then organize it. Do not be afraid to make a badge with 15 or more words. An elaborate badge can be beautiful and highly effective.

The three most obvious candidates for badge content are the name, the brand mark, and the tagline. If you do not have a tagline, a short descriptor can be helpful. You can research the company to write your own two- or three-word tagline. Many times when building a badge for a brand, I have written a memorable tagline that the company has decided to use in other media placements.

Another item to explore is balance words. Balance words are words that are the same length visually, so they balance each other when placed on each side of a badge.

Examples are:
+ Established dates ex: "ESTD" and "2023"
+ Trademark ex: "TRD" and "MRK"
+ Location ex: "MPLS" and "MINN"
+ Descriptor words ex: "QLTY" and "CRFT"

Remember that this is your chance to help tell this brand's story. This is an opportunity to infuse the brand with memorability. If you only insert the same balance words on every badge that you design it will defeat the purpose.

Once you have all of the content established, it is time to create a balanced type lock-up. You can build your visual hierarchy at this point. The company name should be the most important element, followed by the brand mark, then the tagline, and lastly the balance words.

OPTION 1

OPTION 2

OPTION 3

OPTION 4

OPTION 5

OPTION 6

External Badge Shape Containers

The external badge shape can play either a huge role or a subtle role depending on how you play it. A circle or an oval is the default and expected solution. That does not mean that it is wrong. It is just more of a neutral solution and may work very well when you have a complex brand mark that needs room to breathe. That said, I always like to explore a shape that is inspired by the geometry of the brand mark.

In the example on the left, the brand mark combines a "W" with a roof shape, creating a chevron pointing up. Each of the shape options here is inspired by the roof shape. Some are more unique than others. When I presented this set of six options to my client, they thought that options 1, 4, and 5 were too similar to the shape of a bottle cap. They wanted something more distinctive and felt that options 2 and 6 were too expected. They absolutely loved option 3. It was unique, but familiar to the brand. It integrated and accentuated the roofline while the curves on the sides matched the center shape, making it sing visually.

Make sure that you take your time when designing a shape container, trying several options. The more you explore, the better chance you have of finding a brilliant solution.

Right:
PDCo Portland Badgehunting Club
2014

How to Use Shape Containers

When badge design is first explored, the most expected solution is to wrap typography in a circle around the outside of the shape. There is nothing wrong with this, but it is only one of many ways to organize your typography and your information hierarchy. A different way I love to sort typography and iconography is by using shape containers. You can create any shape you like, but I like to explore shapes that are inspired by the geometry of the brand mark. I prefer the shapes to be symmetrical and well balanced.

When creating your shape containers, start by organizing all of your content by size and importance. Then figure out how to visually balance it. Now that you know the general shapes and sizes of the content, you can start to create the shape containers so that they hold the visual content in an aesthetically pleasing manner.

In this example, I used an overlapping effect with my shapes to create another shape that was the perfect container for the word "club."

WEST COAST MAKERS & MINERS

THE

Portland

CLUB NUMBER FOURTEEN

PDX  USA

BADGE
HUNTING

TRADEMARK PROCESSED IN THE UNITED STATES OF AMERICA

TRADE MARK
PENDING
USA

THE

Seattle

BADGEHUNTING

Club

ESTD
2014

Visual Balance

The secret to creating a strong badge is visual balance. Ten words organized poorly can be a chore to read. You want to create something visually exciting that makes someone want to read every word in the order you prescribed. To do that you need to create visual balance.

Just like you learned in algebra class, everything on the left side of the badge should be balanced with an element on the right side. If you do not have a word, balance the badge by using an icon. It is also important to give each element room to breathe. This is usually called padding or negative space. Not only should you balance the element, you should balance the negative space. You are creating a beautiful visual dance. It should have a lovely rhythm that causes joy at a glance.

If you feel like you cannot create a visual balance with the elements you have, perhaps you should add a few more elements. Remember that you are making the rules. Make sure that the rules work in your favor.

Logo Systems with Badges

Not every logo system should incorporate a badge into its brand identity system. For example, for many tech companies a badge would feel out of place in their brand identity system. My advice is not to force a badge into a brand identity system. Instead, let it feel like a natural extension of the brand you are creating. Make sure that you only add a badge to your system if it feels like it strengthens the brand identity.

If you are trying to sell a client on the idea of a badge design, there are two strategic reasons to include one, and knowing these will help you to make your sale. The first is that a badge offers an opportunity to tell a story through both words and visuals. A memorable logo is a successful logo.

The second reason is that you can use the extra space to help explain the function of the brand. The City of Shoreview example shown here has both a version of the logo with "City of Shoreview" and a version with "Shoreview." The shorter "Shoreview" version is preferred. However there are situations where the client will require a badge that provides clarity or an explanation of its function. In this example, the City of Shoreview badge is used to denote that a vehicle is a city vehicle or an employee is a city employee. In these cases, they used the "City of Shoreview" version of the badge.

Having a diverse logo system will future-proof the brand, making it functional for years to come.

Chapter 5
Brand Extensions

Let's go back to our example of the client asking you to "make the logo bigger." As I stated previously, in most cases the size of the logo is not the real issue. The real issue is that the branding in the layout is not strong enough. The way to keep your design work "on-brand" is to integrate the geometry of the brand mark into as many brand elements as possible. Integrate it into the patterns, the icons, the badge shape, photo crops, and photo art direction.

A well-designed brand should remind you of the brand mark at every touch point without needing a gigantic logo on each page. Once I began integrating the DNA of the brand mark into all of the other design elements, I have not been asked to "make the logo bigger." Hard to believe, but it is true.

In this chapter, I will explain how I integrate the geometry of a brand mark into patterns, icons, flourishes, custom typography, and illustration.

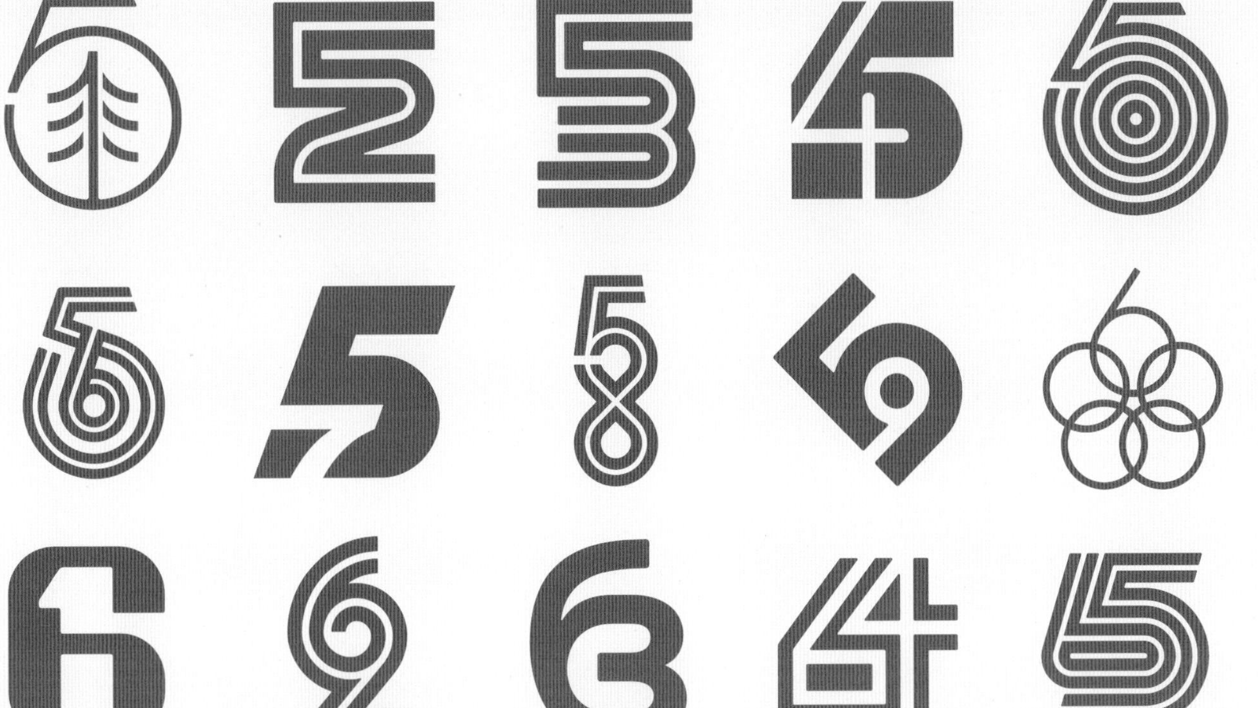

Brand Patterns

Patterns are a tasteful way to add branding to a layout. Patterns are excellent for the top of the brand's Facebook page, the tissue paper a product is wrapped in, or the back of a business card. A good brand pattern should feel like the brand at a single glance. It can be the logo repeated, but it does not need to be. It can be an element from the logo, a series of stripes from a logo, or even the outlined shape of the logo repeated.

When I provide a client with a set of brand patterns, I like to give them a variety of patterns that range from "subtle" to "can't look away." That way the marketing and design teams will have versatility within the system.

In the examples I am sharing here, I show a few different ways that I turned the Peters Design Company logo into a brand pattern. The first example takes the initial spiral established in the brand mark and continues it in an endless spiral. The second example creates a repeating pattern with the brand mark; however, to keep it interesting, I intertwined the shapes to create series of linked logos. The third example takes two of the badges from the brand family and combines them in a pleasing pattern that has an intentionally vintage feel. In the fourth example, the pattern from the first example is used, but I've warped it visually. I created this illusion by printing out the pattern, warping the paper, and photographing a handful of examples.

A large variety is shown here and that is on purpose. This is my company's brand identity and I am intentionally selling my creativity by putting it on display. Not all brands need such a wide variety of patterns. Usually a few complex and a few simple patterns will work perfectly.

Brand Icons

When creating an icon set, first determine your subject matter. Next figure out the simplest way to illustrate each idea. Lastly, skin your icon set with a set of geometric rules established with your brand mark. Your brand mark has a set of rules integrated in the DNA of how it was created.

In the example to the right, the squirrel has the same line width as the brand mark. It also shares the same negative space relationship between the strokes. Additionally, it integrates the same curved shape in a way that illustrates the tail. The circle of the eye is the same shape and size as the center negative space of the brand mark. This squirrel would not feel on-brand for any brand other than Peters Design Company.

That is how you know your icon is doing its job. If you saw this icon without seeing the brand mark, it would make you think of the brand mark, therefore reducing the need for a gigantic logo on each page or layout.

SQUIRREL

MIN   USA

PETERS

DESIGN Cº

MMVIII

Brand Flourishes & Badge Shapes

When creating branded elements like flourishes and badge containers, use the geometry of the brand mark as the blueprint. In the example on the facing page, the badge shape is created using the same positive and negative stroke system established in the brand mark. I have also used subtle rounded corners to give an illusion of motion. When you see the brand mark next to the badge shape they feel like they belong together.

It is important that all of your branded elements feel like they came from the same artist and the same branding system. When designers start pairing a custom logo with a random font and some vector flourishes that they found online, all of the elements feel like a group of strangers forced to live together. This may be the premise of your favorite reality TV show, but it does not work when creating a cohesive brand system. Even if each element is beautiful on its own, they need to feel harmonious together. Creating custom elements allows the design to convey a unified visual language.

Brand Typography

It is rare that a client has the budget to create a custom font. However, when they do, this is your time to shine. Take all of the geometric learnings from the approved brand mark and build a typeface based on this visual-DNA. Match the line widths, the negative space, the curves, and the level of organic versus geometric structure.

When creating a custom font, remember that the true purpose of typography is communication. The font should not only be legible, but should also be a pleasure to read. Many young type designers create fonts that have too much personality and therefore are frustrating to read, especially in long form body copy. As you create letterforms, try them in sentences to test their legibility. I believe a good font should have no more than two or three unique characters that catch your eye. The rest of the font should harmonize with those characters and help them to feel like they belong. An example that is familiar to most designers is the lowercase "a" from the font Helvetica. The Helvetica "a" is pretty sassy and unique, but the font is designed to help the "a" belong as part of the family.

ABCDEFGHIJ
KLMNOºPQR
STUVWXYZ
1234567890

ABCDEFGHIJ
KLMNOºPQR
STUVWXYZ
1234567890

GENUINE

Ⓟ PETERS

We offer a distinctive design aesthetic &
engaging messaging that is both genuine &
thought provoking.

CRAFTED

Ⓟ PETERS

Everything we create
is crafted with care &
excellence in mind.

SPECIAL

Ⓟ PETERS

Everything we create is infused with a
distinctiveness that is uniquely personal
to each of our partners.

ROOTED

Ⓟ PETERS

Our design aesthetic is
influenced by the great
thinkers of the past.

Left:
PDCo Attribute
Poster Series
2016

Brand Illustrations

Brand illustrations add to the visual identity in a similar way to brand icons. Creating branded illustrations is a great way to tell a story for an advertisement, social media, or even an internal facing poster series. Repeatedly using the same memorable brand mark geometry will keep the brand system consistent and memorable. Each element will remind the viewer of the brand mark, strengthening the overall brand identity experience

I begin my illustration work by first sketching out my ideas for each illustration. Next, I apply the geometric learnings from the brand mark to bring my idea to life visually. This works well not only for very simple illustrations like the example to the left, but also with complex and detailed illustrations.

My favorite types of brand illustrations are ones that combine branded vector art with human or product photography. It's a lovely way to integrate the photography into the brand identity package.

Chapter 6
Brand Evolution

You do not need to start from scratch with each logo you design. In fact, it is usually strategically advisable to evolve the current logo. The more times someone sees a logo, the more it sticks in their memory. We call that brand equity. Brand equity can take years of viewing and millions of dollars to become potent. When you start from scratch, you erase all of the visual brand equity. Even ugly logos can become memorable over time.

If you are dealing with a poorly designed logo like the example on the right, there is usually something worth keeping. In this example, I kept the world shape, the colors, and the use of lines to create motion. It feels like an evolution versus a revolution.

If you are dealing with a beautifully designed mark, the refinements can be subtler. Perhaps you could remove a few elements to streamline the design. Simplifying the typography and making it more legible is another great way to evolve an already solid mark.

OLD

NEW

HEARTLAND
TECHNOLOGY

BRAND STANDARDS
MANUAL

2019

What to Focus On?

The best place to start is by asking the client what functional issues they encounter with the current logo. Is it difficult to reproduce because of a gradient? Is the typography hard to read at small sizes? Do the colors clash? Once you know the pain points, you can start to identify solutions that will strategically strengthen the logo.

Next, I like to explore the overall concept. What is the root of the visual idea? Is there a simpler way to express the same thought? Can I shave off an element or two without making it worse?

Last, I like to explore the color. As we discussed in an earlier chapter, color choice needs to be intentional. I ask myself the following questions about the brand's color story. Can I help tell the story better by adjusting the colors? Perhaps making them more saturated to stand out or more neutral to help tell the brand story? Can the idea be expressed with fewer colors? Why depend on four colors when you can tell the same story with two?

To get a better idea of how this flushes out in real life, let's explore a few examples from the Peters Design Company portfolio. I will show the before and after as well as my thoughts behind each logo evolution.

OLD

NEW

OLD

NEW

EXAMPLE:

Urbane Coffee

Urbane started as a mobile espresso bar with the mission of bringing friends and family together over a cup of coffee. As Urbane started to expand and diversify, they needed a brand that reflected their future image. It also needed to be functional and easy to use in all media.

Here's what was not working with the original logo:

+ The icon is worked into the logotype, which reduces legibility.

+ The kerning is awkward and inconsistent.

+ The type choice is outdated.

+ The descriptive typography is too light when reduced to small sizes.

+ The initial "U/Cup" is too thick compared to the rest of the word.

Here's what was working:

+ The "U" + Coffee Cup idea is solid

My solution was to evolve the U/Cup into an icon that could live on its own. I redesigned this icon to make it more ownable and added motion by using multiple lines. This is an example of the visual rhythm technique for combining brand nouns that we discussed in a previous chapter. I also picked a collection of fonts that worked well as a family. Combined, this logo evolution helps to tell the story of a craft-focused coffee shop that puts the customer first.

Hand
CRAFTED

Coffee
CONNECTS

Coffee
IS LOVELY

Sunshine
IN A CUP

OLD

NEW

EXAMPLE:

Eagan Police

When redesigning the brand identity system for the City of Eagan, I had the opportunity to update the logo for the Eagan Police Department. The police chief's request was to update their existing badge so that it would match the new brand identity system.

Here's what was not working with the original logo:
+ Hand-drawn and inconsistent
+ Overly complex and hard to reproduce
+ Too many colors
+ Very thin linework
+ Bad kerning and stretched/squished typography

Here's what was working:
+ It had an official and expected layout for a police badge.
+ The traditional shape is iconic and impactful.

My solution was to take the approved logo that I had created for the City of Eagan and to apply the geometric rules and custom typography to the police badge.

All of the design elements became mono-weight to make it easier to reproduce at small sizes. The wreath shape was replaced with the leaf shape from the Eagan brand mark. I also removed some of the overlapping shapes, like the flags, and could now reduce the symbol from eight colors to three. The result is one of the cleanest police crests in the field. It looks great when applied to the side of the squad cars in metallic gold and silver.

EXAMPLE:

Rush Creek

Rush Creek Church is a multi-campus church in Texas. The church had experienced a large amount of growth and felt that it was time to update their brand identity to reflect their current church family. They were also experiencing issues reproducing their original logo.

Here's what was not working with the original logo:

+ unnecessary gradients
+ The words "rush" and "creek" were closer together than the space between the letters.
+ The brand mark was overly illustrative.
+ The brand name was a phrase, not a name.
+ The font was visually unbalanced.
+ The brand mark did not clearly read as an "R" and "C" or a creek.

Here's what was working:

+ I liked the idea of integrating a creek into an "R."
+ Blue as a color choice made sense with the subject matter.

My solution was to simplify the brand mark and to strengthen the typography. I found overlapping geometry in the leg of the "R" and a rushing creek. Monograms can be confusing in horizontal logos so I decided to use a shape container to clearly separate it from the other typography. I chose a type solution that emphasizes the word "rush," giving the logo motion and life.

OLD

NEW

OUR GOD IS
THREE IN ONE

PUT ON THE
ARMOR OF

LOVE ONE
ANOTHER

Chapter 7
The Shop

The year 2020 was a tough time for most people. The pandemic hit and it hit hard. Many large companies stopped all marketing spending as they waited to see how the market would adapt. Most of the projects that I had in the pipeline evaporated and I had a lot of downtime, which is not a good situation when you are an entrepreneur without paid time off or as many options for government bailouts.

As it has most likely become obvious throughout the course of these pages, I love to design. It's my passion. I can't turn it off. So, with all of my extra time, I decided to start an online shop. I used my time not only to build and promote the shop, but also to create products to sell. In 2020, I designed and uploaded over 100 products. Some of these were designs from the past, but many were brand-new. I learned a lot about merchandise design in a short period of time. In the following pages we will take a look at three of the collections from my shop and the story behind each one.

ALL   612   AMERICA   BIKES   CHRISTIAN   HATS   JACKET   MASKS   NORTH WOODS   POSTERS   SHIRTS   SPACE   VIDEO GAMES

Peace Poster
$30.00

Color Bike Poster
$30.00

Ampersand Poster
$30.00

Speed T-Shirt
$25.00

Speed Poster
$30.00

The Negative Space ABC Poster
$30.00

Americana Collection

On the Fourth of July in America, most folks dress up in patriotic clothing, barbecue a bunch of meat, and head out to see fireworks. The problem is that most of the patriotic clothing available isn't uplifting and fitting for a great nation. I figured it was an excellent opportunity to make some beautiful design work that celebrated my country while increasing access to well-designed Americana clothing.

I started this collection back in 2012 as a Fourth of July social media post and, over the years, continued to develop the marks. With the launch of my shop in 2020 the graphics were ready to go.

There is a tremendous amount of subject matter to work with when exploring the United States' overall brand identity system. There is "America," "USA," stripes, stars, and of course eagles. I am a huge sucker for eagle logos and eagle illustrations. It is truly a majestic bird.

If you are wondering where I find my inspiration for this work, walk through an American antique store. Many of the packages developed at the same time as World War II were and are very patriotic. It was a normal part of the culture to support the war effort. There is a lot of bad design work from this period, but there is also a lot of truly beautiful work. However, you have to dig a bit to find it. Over the years, I have discovered and collected a large number of eagle graphics and often look to them for inspiration when designing a piece for my Americana Collection.

Color Flood Collection

One of my favorite fine artists is Piet Mondrian. He used black lined grids with fills of primary colors to create beautiful compositions. His goal was to create a perfect visual balance between the colors. Several years ago, I began working with a style of illustration and color exploration inspired by Mondrian's black grids and fills of color, dubbing it #shapecolorart. Over the years I have added to my collection of #shapecolorart, and in recent years some of it has made it to the shop as the Color Flood Collection.

One of the more prominent pieces in this collection is a bike poster that I made for a local poster show. A friend of mine, Charles Youel, began this annual poster show called ArtCrank, dedicated to people who love bikes and art. For several years I participated as an artist, designing posters all about my love for biking. You can see the Color Flood Bike Poster at right, and I feature more bike art in the Passion Projects chapter on pages 194–195.

After the success of my Color Flood Bike Poster, I've continued the series with "Peace," "Rose," and "&." They have become some of the most loved pieces of work in my portfolio.

Badgehunting Collection

In 2014, I was working a corporate job downtown and commuting from my home in the suburbs via express bus. I had a 45-minute commute each way and I spent a lot of that time working on freelance projects and fun passion projects.

At the time I was doing a lot of antiquing and searching for vintage design. While on the bus, the idea hit me to start a club devoted to the hunt and I called it Badgehunting. I tagged all of my posts with #badgehunting and I also created a Minneapolis Badgehunting Club logo. Once the Minneapolis chapter crest was posted, my designer friends from across the country asked me to make logos for their cities. Over the next few years, I designed twenty custom #badgehunting logos. After posting them to social media and designing several stickers, I didn't do much with them until 2020. Once I launched the shop, I brought back all of the Badgehunting logos on T-shirts.

Decades into my career as a designer I continue to fill my portfolio with passion projects featuring the type of work that I want to be doing. This specific passion project has brought in a lot of client work over the years and it's a great example of the type of work I love doing.

The real question is, what city should I design next?

Chapter 8
Case Studies

I approach each and every project like it is the most important thing I've ever created. Many of the projects I am sharing in this chapter have had tough moments and difficult feedback. With each, I was able to use the process that I have outlined in this book and the soft skills we have discussed to create a set of brand identity systems that will stand the test of time.

I am sharing a wide range of clients with varying budgets to show you exactly how my process can be adapted and scaled to suit projects of any size. These are all real projects for real clients. Each one was designed with love, care, and respect. Look at these as examples of what you can create using the skills you've acquired in this book.

Let's dig into the stories that made each of these projects special.

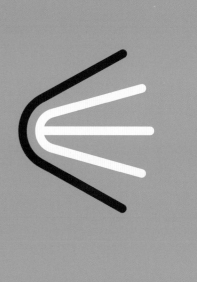

City of Eagan

The City of Eagan is my hometown. We have lived here since 2013. This is where I hike. This is where I explore. This is where I live. I absolutely love it here. When we first moved to Eagan the city had an awful clip art logo and a font that was difficult to read.

When the City of Eagan was founded there was a lone oak in the center of the town. Usually oaks grow in clusters and have the support of each other's roots; however a large singular oak is a sign of independence and strength. The oak has always been a symbol for the City of Eagan and has been represented in some way in each of its logos over the years.

This oak tree that I designed for this logo is symmetrical and fits perfectly in a circle. It is shown on a hill to represent the unique topography of the area. The branches are organic and unique and symbolize the winding streets and cul-de-sacs that add character to the city.

Branding a city comes with many more application concerns than the typical logo project. The final logo needed to work on all kinds of media, from huge wayfinding water towers all the way down to stamped cement garbage cans. Some of the more challenging applications were the city vehicles and the stamped metal city signage.

There is nothing quite as rewarding as seeing your design on the water towers in your hometown. I was truly proud to give Eagan the quality brand identity it deserves.

OLD

NEW

EAGAN MARKET FEST
LOCAL & FRESH

EAGAN ART HOUSE
LIVE CREATIVELY

COMMUNITY CENTER
EAGAN

EAGAN CIVIC ARENA
CA
SPORTS & EVENTS

Freadom

Freadom is an amazing company. They sell clothing, books, cards, and accessories, and all of their net profits are donated to help get books into kids' hands. They have the goal of literacy for all.

I love when client work and passion projects combine. It was such an honor to work on something that I knew was going to do good in the world. Books are so important in childhood development. It helps kids build language skills and exposes them to other cultures and worlds. I see in my own children how much their creativity is inspired by the books we read. Their lives are filled with inspirational stories, and I owe that to the books we have all over our house. So many children do not have access to books and that's just not right. I am so thankful that Freadom is fighting for these kids, and I am thankful that I could help to tell Freadom's story through this brand identity system.

The brand mark that I designed for Freadom combines an eagle, a star, and an open book. The eagle represents freedom. The star represents the individual. The book represents literacy for all.

Due to the nature of Freadom's purpose, this brand mark had multiple functionality concerns, including being embroidered, stamped in plastic, screen printed, engraved in metal, and even pressed into the bottom of ceramic coffee mugs. The result is a mark that is absolutely simple, memorable, and unique and therefore will stand the test of time.

LITERACY · FOR · ALL ·

FREADOM

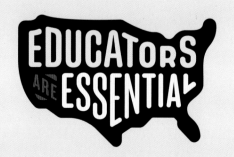

City of Shoreview

After the success of the brand identity system that I created for Eagan, many cities have reached out with logo projects. One of those was the City of Shoreview, Minnesota.

Shoreview's existing logo had many pain points. It used four colors and a gradient that made it extremely difficult to print and impossible to reproduce in one-color variations like engraved metal or embroidery. The thing that stuck out to me was that the dot for the lowercase "i" was in the wrong place. It appears someone forgot to group their elements in Illustrator.

My solution was to take the same subject matter in the old logo and simplify it. This was accomplished by transforming the brand mark from an illustration into a functional logo. My favorite innovation in this mark is the simplified water. It feels like waves washing up on shore and settling as they reach the edge of the lake. The motion and rhythm of the water were captured in three thick lines.

OLD

NEW

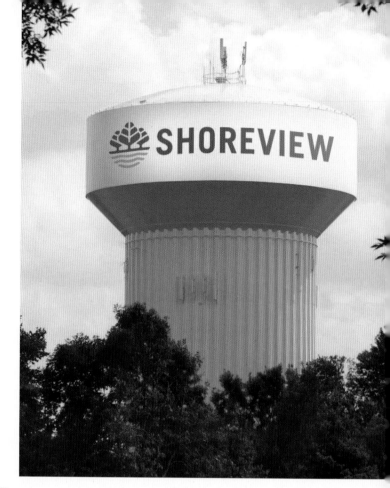

First Free

One of my goals when starting and running my own company was to take on projects that aligned with my passions and beliefs. First Free is my church. I've been a member since 2013. The people at First Free feel like family to me. When Pastor Joel asked if I would be interested in sharing my gifts to help brand the church, I told him to spend the allotted budget on a sweet sign because I would gladly do it for free.

First Free's mission statement is "Christ Centered + Christ Sent." Christ Centered meaning to study the Bible and to look inward. Christ Sent meaning to go spread the word of Christ far and wide. The brand mark that I designed is a direct representation of this mission statement by combining a cross (Christ centered) and a growing tree (Christ sent).

Over the years, I have slowly rebranded every subsection of the church. This was accomplished by designing marks for the children's program, the youth group, and the men's group. I've also had a chance to help with signage, graphics, interior design, and wayfinding. It has been a labor of love.

A friendly and inviting brand identity will draw people in. Being able to use my gifts to serve is a wonderful feeling. In the years since, there has been a huge transformation in our church and I am honored to be a part of that change.

WWW.FIRSTFREECHURCH.ORG

MPLS MINN

FIRST FREE

CHRIST CENTERED + CHRIST SENT

AN EFCA CHURCH

MPLS MINN

FIRST FREE

CHRIST CENTERED + CHRIST SENT

AN EFCA CHURCH

FIRST FREE

CHRIST CENTERED + CHRIST SENT

AN EFCA CHURCH

THE DEEP

WORSHIP + PRAYER

VELOCITY

STUDENT MINISTRIES

CREEKSIDE

KIDS

JOYFUL   GROWTH

AT FIRST FREE CHURCH

CHRIST
CENTERED +
CHRIST SENT
TOGETHER

THE
TR✝UTH

LOVE

City of Hartselle

Hartselle is known as the City of Southern Hospitality. This tagline is important to its citizens as it defines the culture of the city. As its neighboring city Huntsville grows into a tech giant, Hartselle has been growing as well. To reflect the modern nature of their city, they decided to update their municipal building as well as their brand identity system.

My goal with this brand mark was to bring this tagline to life. I captured that friendly nature by showing an "H" that feels joined in a handshake. The result is simple, unique, and friendly. It makes you smile without showing a full-on illustration like the previous logo. I also took the stripes of the awning from the previous mark and reflected them with an inline stroke running through the brand mark.

My partners at Leonard Design, who were responsible for designing the new municipal building, were a pleasure to work with. Joel and Sara would send me notes of encouragement after every meeting. I love working with clients who are cheerful. Their joy is inevitably reflected in the final product.

OLD

NEW

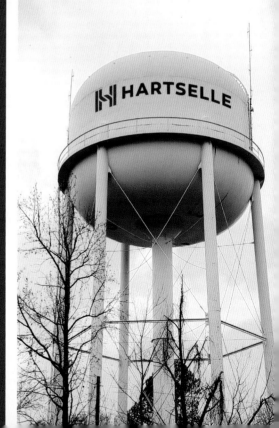

Kwikbit

Sometimes what can seem like challenging feedback can actually make the project stronger—it's all in how you approach the challenge and work to understand where your client is coming from. That was the case with the Kwikbit branding project.

Kwikbit provides gigabit wireless solutions. They needed a mark that could compete with Silicon Valley technology brands. We built them a brand identity system that portrays speed, trust, flexibility, and clarity.

After the initial sketch phase, the client asked me to combine multiple brand marks, specifically sketches 1 and 5 from the next spread. Combining concepts or "Frankensteining Ideas," as it's called in the design business, is usually a horrible idea. In this case, I was able to blend the essence of one sketch with the outer shape of the other. The thoughtful combination makes for a very strong mark that combines speed, technology, and the letter K.

The second piece of challenging feedback was a request for italic typography. I rarely use italic type in logos. Italic type may say "speed," but it definitely does not say technology. I talked to the client and found out that they were hoping the type would feel fast or "kwik." My solution was to create a few diagonal cuts in the typography. The first creates a ligature between the "k" and the "w," eliminating an awkward space between them. The second set of cuts replicate the angle of the "k" with triangular dots for the "i's." The client was very happy with this solution. It now felt fast and high-tech.

In the end, the feedback that could have made for a weak logo actually made the final mark stronger. I identified the actual issues that the feedback was looking to address and fixed them without losing the integrity of the logo.

kwikbit

01

02

03

04

05

06

07

08

09

10

11

12

13

14

15

16

17

18

19

20

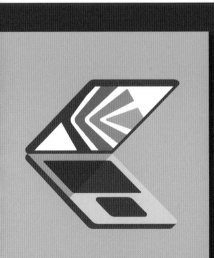

speed is
our priority

kwikbit

New South

New South Outdoor is a growing outdoor advertising company. When they contacted me, they had a logotype that was hard to read and didn't work well in small spaces. This was a huge problem, as their logo is most often used on the frame of the many digital billboards that they own.

New South is a perfect example of why a brand noun list is an invaluable tool in the design process. If you look at most billboard companies, their logo is usually a simple font or a plain monogram. They are completely unremarkable. By digging in with a brand noun list, I found out that my client was interested in investigating a variety of subject matter that would make for a unique mark. Some of the approved brand nouns included ram, star, sunrise, bell, pedestal, and falcon.

The result is one of the most memorable logos that you will see on a billboard. The brand mark evokes travel, new beginnings, power, and rising above the clutter. By completing the edge of the sun in the feathers of the eagle the mark evokes motion and energy. In addition, the full shape forms a circle that fits perfectly in small spaces like mobile and social media.

OLD

NEW

LOGOS THAT LAST / CHAPTER 8 / CASE STUDIES

New South
Brand Manual

 New South

 New South

 New South

Epilogg

Epilogg is the solution to overpriced and impersonal newspaper obituaries. It is a free service that allows you to tell an engaging story about your loved one using words, photos, and video.

I know that an online obituary service does not sound like the flashiest and most enticing project; however, I look at every project as an opportunity to make some of the best work of my career. After all, your next freelance project will be sparked by the latest work that you share. So, it better be good. I truly feel that this is one of the greatest brand identity systems that I have created. It's better than work that I have completed for huge clients like Nike and ESPN. The moral of the story is, every client deserves your best. Don't give up before you start.

The brand noun list for Epilogg included quite a few cheeky ideas that were meant to be humorous, like skulls and gravestones. In the end, we decided to let the humor come from the copy and we let the logo be simple and timeless. The thing with jokes is that they are only funny the first time you hear them. Funny logos are fine for T-shirt graphics, but a long-lasting logo needs to be smart and memorable.

The logo I designed for Epilogg combines an open book and the letter E. Why a book, you ask? Because everyone has a story to tell and Epilogg gives you the freedom to tell your loved one's story.

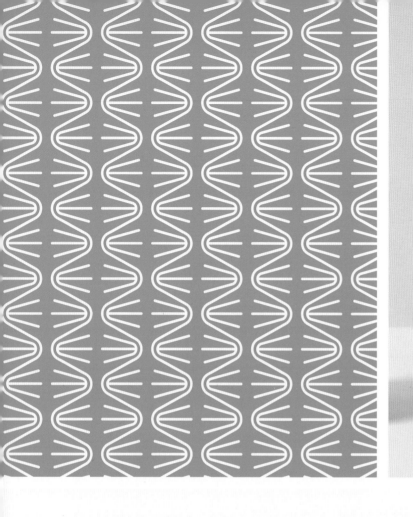

EPILOGG BRAND MANUAL

SAY HELLO
SAY GOODBYE
SAY IT ALL

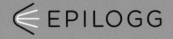

Landmark

Landmark church had a new name and they needed a new brand identity to match. Like all of PDCo's brand identity projects, we started with a brand noun list. This noun list included items that reflected the newly chosen name and messaging that went along with it. Some of the brand nouns on this list were pillar, stone formation, cornerstone, cross, and city on a hill. After sketches were presented, the client chose to develop only one of the 15 options instead of the usual three. They loved the one idea and knew that it perfectly represented their church. The chosen brand mark combined a cityscape, an implied hill, and a cross in the negative space.

When developing the brand book and brand patterns, I decided to work the brand mark into an illustration that amplified its meaning by using multiple aspects of Christian symbolism. First, I incorporated three hills and three rings. The number three is symbolic in Christianity because God is three in one—Father, Son, and Holy Spirit. This illustration places the cross on a hill not only to symbolize Jesus's crucifixion on the cross, but also to reflect this verse from Matthew 5:14: "You are the light of the world. A city that is set on a hill cannot be hidden."

I am incredibly proud of this work. When we dreamt of starting PDCo, Maria and I hoped to work on brands for which we had a passion. Since 2015, we have had the honor of creating brand identity systems for eight churches. There is a deep satisfaction in being able to use my gifts to serve the Lord.

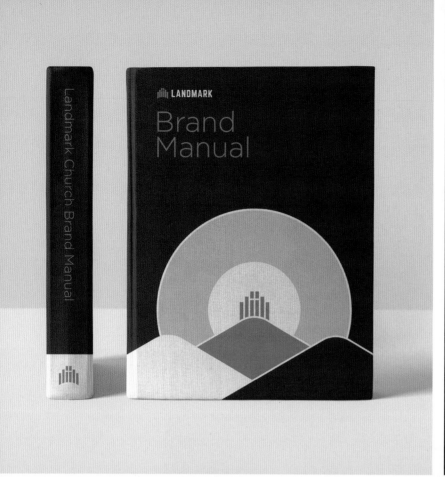

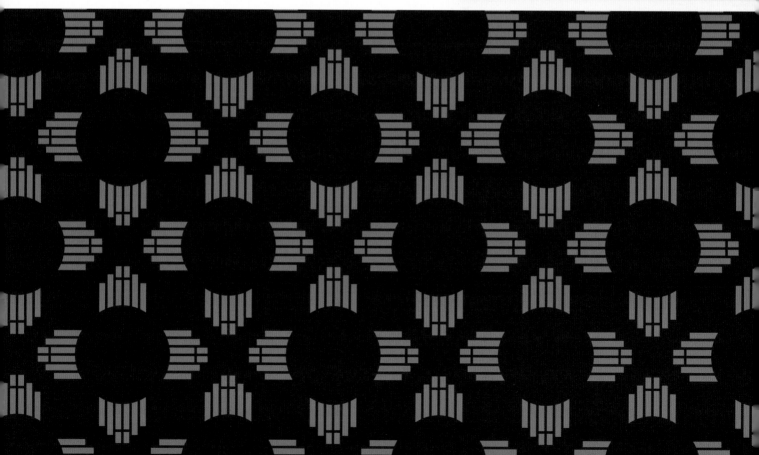

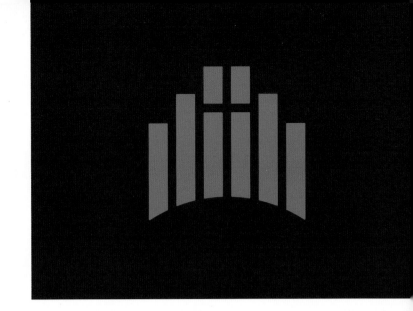

FM

Featherstone Media was growing like crazy and decided to simplify their name to strengthen their image. They bought the URL "FM.net" and hired Peters Design Company to create a new branding system.

With only two letters, the FM logotype itself is small enough to function properly in a social media avatar. The simplified letterforms keep the logo from appearing overtly horizontal in its most compact form. Appearing thicker and more rectangular, they make the overall mark feel balanced and classic. Many timeless marks only use two to four letters, for example: ABC, IBM, Nike, and CNN. On the rare chance you get to design a logo with only two letters in its name, you are set up for victory.

With FM, I presented my usual 15 brand mark options. As usual, there were a range of options, including abstract symbols and monograms that meaningfully combined an F and an M. On the last slide of the deck, I presented the winning mark. The client's eyes immediately lit up. They pointed and said, "That's it." It was one of the quickest logo projects I had ever done. The full logo was there. This freed my time to work on additional brand explorations. The time I normally spent on designing type and making revisions was now used to create brand patterns and mock-ups for a variety of media placements.

Following the brand mark process, I designed the most beautiful (and expensive) business cards I have ever had the opportunity to create. They are printed on black paper stock with green and white foil stamps and are die-cut. These cards are absolutely stunning and worth their weight in gold. Handing out a beautiful business card like this will stop people in their tracks. Rather than being thrown in the trash, it starts a conversation.

Brand Manual　　　FM　　　2020

NOAH
REED
SUPPORT
(800) 560 - 2485
NOAHR@FM.NET
FM.NET

MFT Automation

MFT was shortening their name from Multi Feeder Technology to MFT Automation. They had hired Patrick Hanlon of Primal Branding to help with their brand strategy and he suggested PDCo to handle the brand identity system.

Basically, automation systems are machines that automate simple functions in a factory, like packaging and labeling a frozen pizza. MFT creates custom, problem-solving solutions for their clients by building machines that work fast and flawlessly.

The brand mark options for this project were centered on speed, machinery, and multiple parts assembling into one coordinated system. Because the shorthand of the name (MFT) was so brief, I suggested half logotype solutions and half brand marks that would pair with a logotype. By combining the implication of speed and multiple parts assembling into a gear, the winning brand mark tells the story of the company in a simple and slightly abstract way that makes it timeless. As we discussed earlier in the book, this logo uses implied motion to draw your eye to the center, keeping the focus on the brand mark.

Because the brand mark had so much meaning, I used a logotype solution that was simple so that the brand mark could shine rather than create competing forces.

AUTOMATION

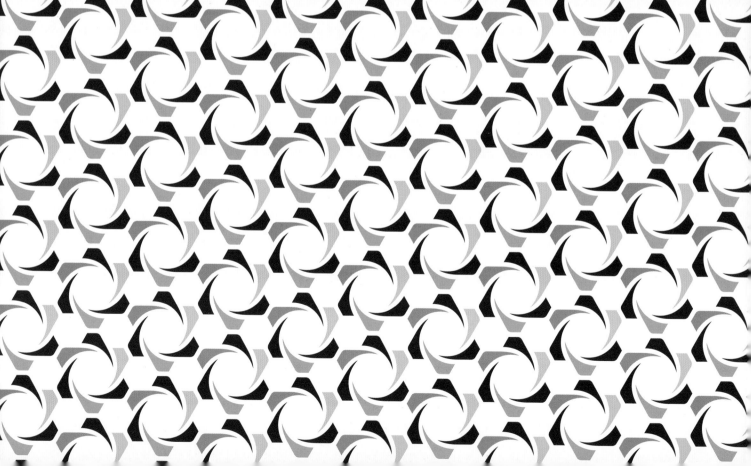

LOGOTYPE OPTIONS

Golden Bear

Golden Bear Equities is a real estate investment firm. They take pride in being a California-based company and chose a name derived from the state's history. Among other things, California is known for its famous gold rush of 1849 and the grizzly bear prominently featured on its state flag.

The brand noun list for Golden Bear included housing and real estate themed nouns as well as California themed nouns. The two brand marks that rose to the top were a "GB" monogram and a golden bear with a house silhouette in the negative space of its legs. The client was having a hard time deciding which to use. Since one of these was a brand mark and the other was a monogram, I suggested that they could be used in tandem.

The trick to using multiple marks is to clearly identify which mark is the primary brand mark and which is secondary. This is a technique commonly used with sports teams and it makes for a playful system with a diverse look and feel.

In 2021, one of my friends from Instagram sent me a photo from the Adobe Max conference. In the photo, the Golden Bear brand identity was prominently featured on the main stage by Adobe Behance. That photo made my day.

GOLDEN
BEAR
EQUITIES

Wits Realty

One day my friend Josh reached out because he and a few of his friends were starting a realty company. Realty companies generally have poorly designed logos. They choose to spend their marketing budgets on billboards and bus bench ads rather than investing in a well-crafted brand identity system. However, Josh understood the invaluable power of design. He understood that every interaction you have with a client makes an impression and those impressions lead to new business. Josh understood that you only get one chance to make an all-important first impression.

I spent my early career dreaming about working on clients like Nike and Patagonia and complaining about the clients I was forced to work on. I quickly learned that you can do inspiring work for any brand no matter how big or small. I feel the brand identity that I created for Wits stands head and shoulders above their competition. I have heard designers say, "That doesn't look anything like a realty brand!" and that was exactly what we were going for with this design. The only way to visually innovate in an industry is to design something different and unexpected.

A realty company's most prominent media placement is its yard sign. This is another place where realty companies traditionally go cheap and expected. I convinced Josh and his team to make their signs feel luxurious. We accomplished this idea with stained wood posts center cut with multiple, modular metal inserts.

The unique and innovative design system we created helped Wits stand out from the pack. Combined with their strong customer service and quality staff, they've grown and thrived.

Chapter 9
Passion Projects

My first graphic design teacher, John DuFresne was a tough cookie. On the first day of class he sat all of us down for a talk. He said, "Being a graphic designer is hard. If you took this class because you thought it would be easy to make simple little logos, you're fooling yourself. To be a successful designer, you're going to have to work harder and longer than most doctors. Anyone who does not have a real passion for graphic design needs to march out of this room right now and go switch your major."

John was right. Passion is the fuel that drives the best design work. You are always going to push yourself a little more if your heart is in it.

One thing I have hammered home in this book is that it is important to fill your portfolio with the type of work that fuels your passion. Often that can be hard to do, especially if you are working at an agency with a strong-minded creative director. If you are not getting the opportunities to do the quality and type of work you are capable of at your place of business, then you need to do it on the side. Look for opportunities to use your gifts to help others while you fine-tune your portfolio.

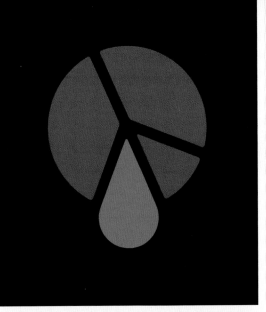

MINNESOTA & WISCONSIN
ANGLERS
Club

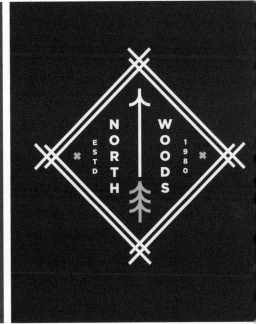

NORTH WOODS
ESTD 1980

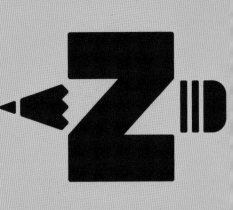

North Woods Anglers Club

When I was a kid, I really didn't like to fish. I thought it was boring. I would sit in the front of the boat and daydream. It was not until my dad took me to the Boundary Waters Canoe Area when I was a young teen that I started understanding the appeal. The secret to having a good time fishing is a two-part answer. First, fish with good company. Second, you will have more fun if you're catching lots of fish, especially if they are big.

In my life I have spent lots of time on the water with my dad and my boys. Some of my favorite days on the water did not involve any fish at all. What I remember were the conversations. I remember singing Beatles songs in the Canadian backwoods with my dad. I also remember the time he broke a rib on the second day of a two-week trip and soldiered through the remaining ten days without complaining (much).

I've also had the privilege of catching thousands of fish in my lifetime. Among those are a 46-inch northern pike along with a 40-inch muskie that I caught with my bare hands while swimming with my family. Catching a trophy fish gives me the same thrill I get when designing a perfect negative space logo. Both take a long time and a lot of effort, and both are absolutely worth the work.

I decided to take all the passion I have for fishing and apply it to a line of hats, tees, and prints for my shop. This collection was illustrated plein air in a pocket sketchbook while on a fishing trip in Voyageurs National Park.

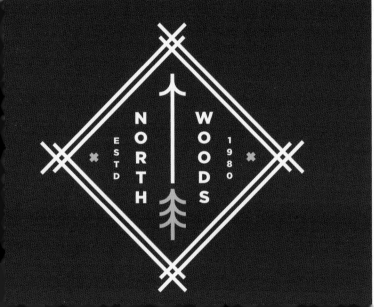

Peace in Ukraine

I have Ukrainian blood running in my veins, so when I heard that on February 24, 2022, Russia had invaded Ukraine I was devastated. I wanted to help convince people that war was not the answer. It never is. The invasion has resulted in tens of thousands of deaths on both sides.

In response, I did what I always do when I want to lend a hand. I made art. I made art about peace and art about my feelings. I made art about unity and love. The work helped me to process my thoughts. After I shared the work on social media, many victims from Ukraine reached out to say thank you and shared my images to reach an even larger audience.

I truly believe artwork can change the world. As designers, we have great power and a huge responsibility. If we only use our gifts to serve giant corporations, we will never make the positive impact we are capable of.

Camp

In 2019, my family and I embarked on an epic tour of the northern national parks. We hit Yellowstone, Grand Tetons, Devils Tower, the Badlands, and Mount Rushmore. It was a thrilling adventure for our three boys and us. The best parts of the trip came when we would get off the beaten path and edge a bit into the wilderness. It did not take long to get away from the crowds and find God's beauty in the quiet of nature.

While my boys played in the woods after a picnic in Yellowstone, I had an idea for a brand that was also a call to action. It would be called "Camp." The name could be used on its own or to promote the different parks, such as a T-shirt reading "Camp Yellowstone." I sketched the idea on a paper napkin using a tent as the "A" to be a simple nod to the meaning of the design. The logotype is intentionally created to be used on its own or in headlines. This functionality helped to dictate its shape container and font.

A year or two later I was sitting at my desk when I remembered my idea for Camp. I immediately set to work building out the system. I posted my initial brand launch idea on LinkedIn and had multiple offers to buy the system or to go into business building the brand as partners. That's how you know you have struck gold.

CAMP
Badlands
NATIONAL PARK
U.S.A

CAMP
Acadia
NATIONAL PARK
U.S.A

CAMP

Justice for George Peace for America

Justice & Peace

I spent over 33 years of my life in South Minneapolis. I was born there. I went to South High School there. I fell in love there. To me, it's home, although our story together is not all roses and rainbows. I was robbed at knifepoint there. My wife was robbed at gunpoint there. I was shot there. Yet, we continue our love affair. We had our first two kids there. We bought our first house there. We started our business there. In 2020, I hated seeing my hometown burned and destroyed. I love Minneapolis. I care for my country.

Watching George Floyd murdered made me cry like a baby and I don't cry. Seeing the look in that officer's murdering eyes filled me with rage. The kind of rage that I felt when I attacked the thieves who put a gun to my wife's head in 2009. I protected her that night, but found myself in the ICU at HCMC. People kept telling me that I should get a gun and asking me, "Don't you want revenge?" I have found peace and grace in Jesus Christ. I don't want a gun because I don't want to be a murderer. What I want is peace. I want peace in Minneapolis. I want peace in America.

From this place of love and a longing for peace, I created the Justice for George: Peace for America collection for my shop. All of the proceeds from this line of merchandise were donated to the One Fund. The One Fund exists to support African American churches and ministries whose communities were impacted by the 2020 crisis in Minneapolis.

My Boys

One of the joys of having children and being a designer is that you get to share your love for them with the world in a beautifully designed birth announcement. For each of my four boys I crafted a unique design as a special gift to them.

Matthew's birth announcement has a royal crest feel to it through its flowing banners, shields, crowns, and 55 organized words contained in a balanced badge. This work is intricate, with each word chosen and placed with care.

Luke's announcement is bolder and brighter to match the meaning of his name: bringer of light. With this birth announcement, I began with the typography of Luke's name. Once it was crafted, I built my way out from the middle. Each element was custom designed to match the custom typography.

Josh's birth announcement has a much more organic feel to it. I wanted it to feel alive. His name has a double meaning of "Yahweh is salvation" and "new life." Every bit of this design feels like it's growing. I custom designed the typography so that the "J" and the "A" would be mirror images of each other. I replaced each of the ball terminals with leaves. And I applied a very traditional inline pattern to give it a feeling of history.

Last is Archer's announcement. His name comes from Psalm 127: 3-5: "Children are a heritage from the Lord, offspring a reward from him. Like arrows in the hands of a warrior are children born in one's youth. Blessed is the man whose quiver is full of them." His announcement was simplified into a symbol that combines a bow and arrow, an "A," and a cross.

JOYOUS SPIRIT
FEAR OF GOD · LOVE OF GOD
ALLAN & MARIA PETERS
Welcome
BORN MAY 29th 2010
MATTHEW
LONNIE·PETERS
8 · 20
Ora
GIFT FROM GOD
HUMILITY & STRENGTH · HONESTY & INTEGRITY
RAISED WITH LOVE
EIGHT POUNDS · EIGHT OUNCES · TWENTY & THREE QUARTERS INCHES
PETERS · MALCOLM

HONESTY · INTEGRITY
SEPT
9lb 8oz · BORN 10 2012 22nd
ALLAN & MARIA PETERS WELCOME
LUKE
ALLAN·PETERS
BRINGER OF LIGHT
MPLS · MADE IN THE USA · MINN
PETERS · MALCOLM

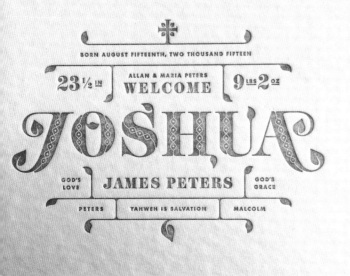

BORN AUGUST FIFTEENTH, TWO THOUSAND FIFTEEN
ALLAN & MARIA PETERS
23½ IN   WELCOME   9 LBS 2 OZ
JOSHUA
GOD'S LOVE   JAMES PETERS   GOD'S GRACE
PETERS · YAHWEH IS SALVATION · MALCOLM

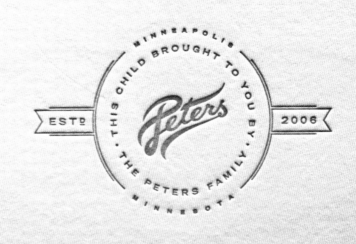

MINNEAPOLIS
· THIS CHILD BROUGHT TO YOU BY ·
ESTD   Peters   2006
· THE PETERS FAMILY ·
MINNESOTA

· ARCHER · PETERS ·
· JONATHAN ·
· BORN IN EAGAN MINNESOTA ON SEPTEMBER 20TH 2021 ·
8.5 POUNDS · 21.5 INCHES

Left:
Bicycle Prints
2010-2021

Bikes

I grew up biking. When I was young, my father would haul my sister and me in a bike trailer all around Minneapolis. As soon as I had the training wheels taken off my Huffy at age six, I was hooked. The feeling of the wind in your hair as you ride down a steep hill is intoxicating. There is nothing quite like that sense of speed created by your body, a metal frame, and a pair of wheels. I find solitude in my life when the only sound is the whistling of wind passing by my ears as I fly down a hill.

When I started working in downtown Minneapolis, I'd bike to work all summer. The daily exercise really got my creative juices flowing in the morning. During those quiet commutes I would have time to think through my day and also learned that the best ideas usually come when you have undistracted time to yourself.

Now that I'm in my forties, I usually bike around Eagan with my kids. I encourage them to push themselves up the big hills and embolden them to take the less beaten paths. We love to bike through obscure neighborhoods looking for garage sales or remote parks.

Over the years, as my life has changed, my relationship with my bike has also changed. In the art I've created about biking, you can see that change. I have prints about city life, creativity, and having babies. I'm excited to see where life takes me next. I only hope it takes me there on a bike.

Negative Space Alphabet

In 2021, I decided to participate in the 36 Days of Type challenge. In this challenge you create a number or a letter of the alphabet each day until the 36 days are up. I also decided to add a story to each letter by utilizing the power of negative space. Some executions came out better than others, but overall, I was happy with the result. For those 36 days, this was my morning logo exercise program. I'd start each day designing my letter and then I'd be ready to rock for my client projects.

Some of these took serious thought. How do you create a symbol out of the negative space of an L? How about a "1"? I had to get tricky in order to create a consistent system and found the solution was to break into the geometry of the shape's interior.

In the end, I was able to explore my love of typography and negative space all while promoting our company on social media. As a bonus, the designs could be combined to create a print that works perfectly in a child's bedroom, a win-win I didn't see coming when I took the challenge.

LOVING ALL PEOPLES

Loving All Peoples

Kyle Jenkins runs a church in Dallas, Texas, that is committed to following the mandate of Jesus to love, serve, and reach all people. When Kyle originally reached out, Loving All Peoples was small and did not have the budget for a full-blown logo assignment. The thing is, I really liked Kyle when I talked with him and was blown away by what they were doing in Dallas. They were truly changing lives.

When I heard the name and mission of the church, I immediately imagined a brand mark that used the shape of a heart to create the initials of the church. I did a quick pencil sketch of my idea and texted it to Kyle. He took one look and gave me the thumbs-up.

To be honest, I designed this project for a fraction of my normal fee. I truly felt that God put this project into my hands and put that idea into my head because He wanted me to help Kyle and his church.

This logo has not only helped Kyle's church, but has also gone on to bring in several new clients to PDCo. It has had thousands of hits on Instagram and Behance because it is simple, clever, and easy to share. It's a logo that looks so incredibly simple anyone could think of it, but instead it is an idea that was waiting for just the right client.

Top Left:
X-Ray Photocopy

Top Right:
PDCo City Life Poster
2009

Bottom:
PDCo Pencil Pistol Poster
2010

Fearless

When my wife, Maria, turned 26, we had a party for her at our home in South Minneapolis. Later that evening we were robbed by masked thieves in our backyard. In this frightening exchange, I was shot through my flank. The bullet entered between my ribs and traveled through the liver, gallbladder, large and small intestines, and, the worst part, two major arteries. I was in the hospital for many days. It was a terrifying and miserable time, not only for me, but also my entire family. I thank the Lord God that I am still here today.

This was the turning point in my life. It taught me that your time on earth is limited and you should use it wisely. It also taught me not to be afraid of other people. I do not mean physically. Most bad design is created by fear-based decisions. Creatives worry about what the client will think. The client worries about what their boss will think. The boss worries about what the customer will think. Fear does nothing positive for design.

Making fearless decisions will turn a good idea into an excellent idea. People will follow a bold leader because they bring clarity and direction to a project.

This experience also gave me a platform. People from across the country heard about the shooting and asked me to come speak at places like Facebook, AIGA National, and Disney. I was finally in the place I needed to be to make a positive influence on the world of design. I had a new outlook on life and a new approach to all my relationships. My career took off and opportunities opened everywhere.

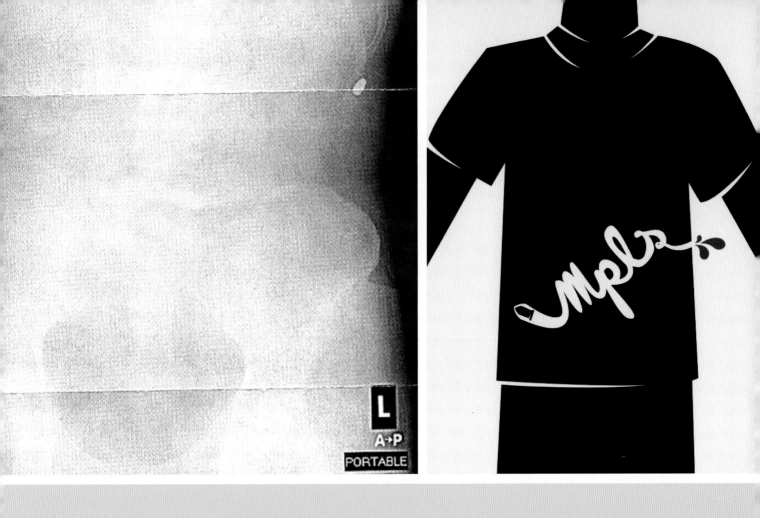

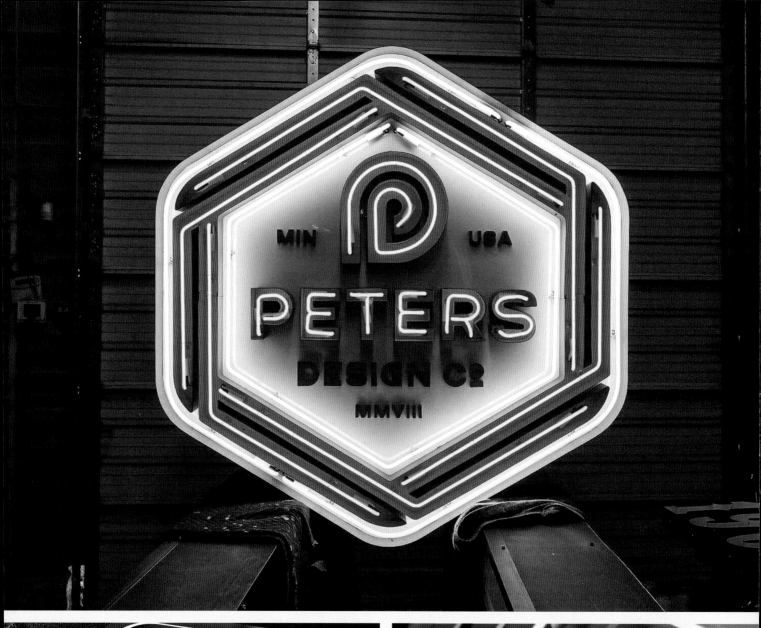

Thank You

I hope you enjoyed the chance to go swimming in my brain for 200-plus pages. It is my goal in sharing my design insight and brand mark process that you would take that which applies and build pieces of what I have shared into your own workflow. Writing this book has been a bucket list item for me since the day I read *Paul Rand* by Steven Heller. When I finished Heller's book, I thought to myself, "This is the pinnacle of a career." I decided then and there that I would work my butt off in order to fill a book with work that was of a high enough caliber to be viewed in the same light as some of my design heroes. Along the way, I discovered that I wanted to teach and share what I have learned. Rather than teaching a college class of only 20 to 30 students, I decided that a book could double both as a collection of my work and as an educational tool to help professionals understand how I do what I do.

You might be asking, "What's next for PDCo?" or "Is this it?" Honestly, this is just the beginning. I do not feel like I've reached my pinnacle of potential. My best work is yet to come. I consider myself a student for life, always learning and adapting my process.

I would love to write a second book all about badgehunting. In an ideal world, we would take three to six months off and travel the country exploring small-town museums, antique stores, and estate sales looking for the most beautiful vintage examples of badges, brand marks, and typography. The book would be organized by region to follow both our adventures and our findings.

If you'd like me to visit for a lecture or workshop, shoot me an email (allan@allanpeters.com) or DM (instagram: @allanpeters). It's one thing to read a book, but it's another to get your hands dirty making projects together.

Acknowledgments

I want to thank my wife and partner, Maria Peters, first. She is the person who lit the fuse for this project originally. Pretty much all of the best things in my life I can trace back to her. I also want to thank both Maria and my father, Mark Peters, for reading and editing my book. They helped me take my rough draft and craft it into its final form. I also want to thank my children for having patience with me as I wrote this book over the past six months.

Thank you to my publisher, Rockport, and to my acquisitions editor, Jonathan Simcosky, for seeking me out and turning my dream into a reality. I also want to thank my art director, Anne Re, for answering all of my production questions and for making my final files shine.

Most importantly, I would like to thank God. He's the artist who made all of the artists. Thank you for making me a brushstroke in your great masterpiece.

About the Author

Allan Peters is the partner and chief creative officer of Peters Design Company. At PDCo he has partnered with brands such as Nike, Amazon, and Patagonia. His work has been recognized internationally by numerous award shows and magazines, including Clio, *Communication Arts*, and *How* Magazine. He is a lover of handcrafted vintage and antique goods and comes alive when scouring small-town antique malls and swap meets. In his free time, he can be found biking with his four boys around the city.

Index

Page numbers in *italics* indicate photos and illustrations.

A

abstract logos, memorability of, 37
Americana Collection, *122,* 123
Ampersand Print, PDCo, *2*
apple, combined with heart, 56, *57*
Armor of God, PDCo, *54,* 55
ArtCrank poster show, 124
artwork
    compositional movement in, 59
    passion for, 26
    power of, 187
    universally beautiful, 29

B

badge design process, 80
    content organization, 82, *83*
    external badge shape containers, *84,* 85
    how to use shape containers, 86, *87*
    logo systems with badges, 90, *91*
    visual balance, *88,* 89
badgehunting, 69, 70, *71–79,* 127, 203
Badgehunting Collection, *126,* 127
badges
    PDCo, *81, 98*
    purpose of, 90
    shape of, 99
    unique, *72–73,* 73
balance words, for badges, 82
Bass, Saul, 70
beauty, universal, 29
Behance, 30, 69, 174, 199
Between the Lines, PDCo, *8*
Bicycle Poster, Color Flood, 124, *125*
bicycles, *194,* 195
billboards, 154
birth announcements, *15, 192, 193*
black, in color palettes, 34
blue, as common logo color, 34
books
    on brand identity design, 7, 203
    child development and, 134
    in Epilogg logo, 158, *159–61*
brand equity, 104

brand evolution. *See* logo evolution
brand extensions, 92
    flourishes and badge shapes, *98, 99*
    icons, 96, *97*
    illustrations, *102,* 103
    patterns, *94,* 95
    typography, 100, *101*
Brand Mark Designs, PDCo, *40*
brand mark exploration, in logo design process, *43*
brand mark presentation, first-round, 62
brand mark revisions, *64,* 65. *See also* case studies; logo evolution
brand marks
    for badges, 82
    bold, 74, *74–75*
    uses for, 80
brand noun lists, 45, 56, 62, 154, 158, 162, 174
brand noun process, as logo design step, *42,* 44–45
brand noun recap, at presentation stage, 62
brand nouns, combining, *42,* 48–59, 111
brand system
    components of, 80
    in logo design process, *43*
business cards, FM, 166, *168, 169*

C

Camp, 188, *189*
case studies, 7, 128, *129*
    City of Eagan, 130, *130–33*
    City of Hartselle, 146, *146–49*
    City of Shoreview, 138, *138–41*
    Epilogg, 158, *159–61*
    First Free, 142, *143–45*
    FM, 166, *167–69*
    Freadom, 134, *135–37*
    Golden Bear, 174, *175–77*
    Kwikbit, 150, *151–53*
    Landmark, 162, *163–65*

    MFT Automation, 170, *171–73*
    New South, 154, *154–57*
    Wits Realty, 178, *179–81*
Cash Cuffs, PDCo, *23*
City Life Poster, PDCo, *201*
City of Eagan, *129*
    case study, 33, 130, *130–33*
    logo process, *64,* 65
    police badge, *114,* 115
City of Hartselle, *129*
    case study, 146, *146–49*
City of Shoreview, *58,* 59, *129*
    badge, 90, *91*
    case study, 138, *138–41*
clients
    brand mark presentation to, 62
    building relationship with, 66
    choosing, 22, 25
    marketing budgets of, 22
    product quality of, 25
    revision feedback from, *64,* 65, 92, 150
color
    choosing, 34, 108
    purpose of, 34
Color Flood Bicycle Poster, 124, *125*
Color Flood Collection, 124, *125*
Color Flood Peace Poster, 124, *125*
Color Flood Rose Poster, 124, *125*
color palette, as pillar of logo longevity, 34
combining brand nouns, in logo design process, *42,* 48–59, 111
company name, on badges, 82
competitive analysis, for choosing color, 34
compositional movement, 59
content organization, in badge design process, 82, *83*
Craftsmanship, PDCo, *32*
Creative Vision, PDCo, *20*
Creativity, PDCo, *58*
Creekside Kids, *67*
custom typography, 65, 76, *76–77,* 100, 115

D

Daydream Brewery, PDCo, *54*
Dribbble, 30, 69
DuFresne, John, 182

E

Eagan. *See* City of Eagan
eagle graphics, 123, 154, *155–57*
Eames Lounger, 9
embroidery, for testing functionality, 33
Epilogg, *129*
    case study, 158, *159–61*
    logo process, *60*
external badge shape containers, *84, 85*

F

fearless decisions, 66, 200
Firecraft Pizza, 52, *53*
First Free case study, 142, *143–45*
Fitch, Luis, 14
flourishes, brand, 99
Floyd, George, 191
FM case study, 166, *167–69*
fonts. *See* typography
forgettable logos, 37
Freadom, *53, 129*
    case study, 134, *135–37*
functionality, as pillar of logo longevity, 33
funny logos, 158

G

Golden Bear, *53*
    case study, 174, *175–77*

H

Hand in Hand, PDCo, *58*
Hardin Valley
    brand nouns, 45
    logo options, *63*
    sketches, *46*
Hartselle. *See* City of Hartselle
hats, brand mark on, 29
Healthy Earth, PDCo, *24*
heart, combined with apple, 56, *57*
Heartland Technology, 104, *105–7*
Heller, Steven, 7, 203
Helvetica font, 100
Herron, Mychal, 12
horizontal logos, 80, 116

I

icons, as brand extension, 96, *97*
illustrations, as brand extension, 103
    PDCo, *102*
Industrio (design studio), 14
Initio (design studio), 13–14
inspiration sources, 18, 69–70, *71–79, 72, 74, 76, 78,* 123
Instagram, 69, 199
internet searches, for design originality, 30
italic type, 150

J

Jenkins, Kyle, 199
Jet Financial, *53*
Justice & Peace, *57, 183, 190,* 191

K

Kwikbit, *129*
    case study, 150, *151–53*

L

Landmark case study, 162, *163–65*
large spaces, brand mark for, 80
letterforms, in FM logotype, 166, *167–69*
lightning bolt, combined with shield, 48, *49*
lines
    overly thin, 33
    thickness of, 61
    for visual rhythm, *54,* 55
linework, for visual flow, 59
locations, for inspiration hunting, 70
Loewy, Raymond, 33
logo design
    common problems in, 33, 47
    long-lasting, 9, 10 (*see also* pillars of logo longevity)
    testing, 33
logo design process
    of Peters Design Company, 7, 38, 41
    steps in, *42–43*
        brand noun process, *42,* 44–45
        combining brand nouns, *42,* 48–59
        presentation to client, 62
        revisions and client guidance, *64,* 65
        selling mark to client, 66
        sketch phase, *42, 46,* 47
        vectorizing & gridding, *43, 60,* 61

logo evolution, 104, 108
    examples
        City of Eagan police badge, *114,* 115
        Heartland Technology, 104, *105–7*
        North Stars, *109*
        Rush Creek, 116, *117–19*
        Urbane Coffee, *110,* 111, *112–13*
logotypes
    Camp, 188, *189*
    FM, 166, *167–69*
    MFT Automation, 170, *172, 173*
Love of Learning, 56, *57*
Loving All Peoples, *198,* 199

M

marketing budget, as pillar of logo longevity, 22
McDonald's logo, 22
McNulty, EJ, 14
memorability
    of classic brand marks, 37
    of logos, 90, 104
    simplicity and, 38
    time creating, 21, 104
MFT Automation, *129*
    case study, 170, *171–73*
Minneapolis, 191
Minneapolis Badgehunting Club, PDCo, *83, 126,* 127
Mondrian, Piet, 124

N

national parks, 188, *189*
Nature Exploration, PDCo, *50*
negative space
    on badges, 89
    in brand icon, 96
    for combining brand nouns, 48
    line thickness and, 61
    tight, 33
Negative Space Alphabet, *183,* 196, *197*
negative space logos, 52, *53, 58,* 59
New South, *129*
    case study, 154, *154–57*
Nike Swoosh, 18, 21, 37
North Stars, *39, 109*
North Woods Anglers Club, *183,* 184, *185*
Number Set, PDCo, *93*

O

oak tree symbolism, 130
originality, as pillar of logo longevity, 30
overlapping geometry, 48, *50,* 51, 116

P

passion projects, 182, *183*
    Bicycle Prints, *194,* 195
    birth announcements, 192, *193*
    Camp, 188, *189*
    client work and, 134
    Fearless, 200, *201*
    Justice & Peace, *190,* 191
    Loving All Peoples, *198,* 199
    Negative Space Alphabet, 196, *197*
    North Woods Anglers Club, 184, *185*
    Peace in Ukraine, *186,* 187
patriotic design inspiration, 123
patterns
    as brand extension, 95
    PDCo, *94,* 95
Paul Rand (Heller), 7, 203
PDCo Shop, 120, *121*
    collections
        Americana Collection, *122, 123*
        Badgehunting Collection, *126,* 127
        Color Flood Collection, 124, *125*
        Justice for George: Peace for America, *190,* 191
Peace in Ukraine, *183, 186,* 187
Peace Poster, Color Flood, *35,* 124, *125*
Peace Star, PDCo, *28*
Pencil Pistol Poster, PDCo, *201*
Pencil Potion, PDCo, *31*
personal passion, as pillar of logo longevity, 26
Peters, Allan, *6, 11, 13, 15,* 68, *131, 193, 205*
    background of, 7, 9–10, 12–15, 191
    bicycles and, 195
    client relationships and, 66
    early drawings of, *13,* 15
    online shop of (*see* PDCo Shop)
    passion projects of (*see* passion projects)
    shooting of, 191, 200
Peters, Maria, 7, 13–14, 15, 162, *193,* 200
Peters Design Company
    about, 16
    founding of, 7, 15, 16

future of, 203
    logo design process of, 7, 38, 41
    neon sign, *6, 202*
    sign and hat, *17*
pillars of logo longevity, 18
    color palette, 34
    functionality, 33
    marketing budget, 22
    originality, 30
    personal passion, 26
    product quality, 25
    simplicity, 38
    story, 37
    time, 21
    universal beauty, 29
Portland Badgehunting Club, PDCo, 86, *87, 126*
product quality, as pillar of logo longevity, 25
pursuit of perfection, in logo design, 10

R

Rand, Paul, 70
realty company logos, 178
    Wits Realty, 178, *179–181*
red, as common logo color, 34
revisions and client guidance, *64,* 65
Rose Poster, Color Flood, *27,* 124, *125*
Rush Creek logo evolution, 116, *117–19*

S

Safe, PDCo, *19*
Seattle Badgehunting Club, PDCo, *88*
shape containers
    external badge, *84,* 85
    how to use, 86
shapes, badge, *72–73,* 73
Shell logo, 33
shield, combined with lightning bolt, 48, *49*
Shooting Star, PDCo, *36*
Shoreview. *See* City of Shoreview
simplicity
    for functionality, 33
    vs. originality, 30
    as pillar of logo longevity, 38
sketches, variations in, 61
sketch phase, of logo design process, *42, 46,* 47
small spaces, brand mark for, 80
spaceship drawings, 12, *13*
squirrel icon, PDCo, 96, *97*
Starry Night (van Gogh), 29
start-up companies, 22, 25
Stay Home. Stay Safe, PDCo, *57*

Storm Damage Solutions, *49*
story, as pillar of logo longevity, 37

T

taglines, 82, 146
Target, 15
Texas Wine Club, *57*
36 Days of Type challenge, 196, *197*
time, as pillar of logo longevity, 21
Transparency, PDCo, *54, 58*
T-shirts
    badgehunting logo, *126,* 127
    Camp Yellowstone, 188, *189*
Type Fight P, PDCo, *54*
typography
    alternative to italic, 150
    custom, 65, 76, *76–77,* 100, 115
    negative space and, 196, *197*
    PDCo, *101*
    revising, 65
    shape containers and, 86, 116

U

unexpected twists, 48, 56, *57*
universal beauty, as pillar of logo longevity, 29
Uno (design studio), 14
Urbane Coffee logo evolution, 11, *110,* 111, *112–13*

V

van Gogh, Vincent, 29
vectorizing & gridding, in logo design process, *43, 60,* 61
vertical logos, 80
visual balance
    for badges, *88,* 89
    for universal beauty, 29
visual flow, 48, *58,* 59
visual overlap, 52
visual rhythm, 48, *54,* 55, 111

W

white, in color palettes, 34
Wits Realty, *129*
    case study, 178, *179–81*
    logo process, *84,* 85
World War II era design, 123

X

X-ray photocopy, *201*

Y

yard signs, realty company, 178, *181*